ARE YOU COMPETITIVE?
RESOURCEFUL?
GLORY HUNGRY?
COURAGEOUS?

If you are, *Sneaky Feats* is the manual for you
—the parlor performer's practical guide to the
crafty art of conspicuous behavior. Learn how
to:

LASSO AN ICE CUBE (don't knock it
   till you've tried it).
MAKE THE WORLD'S NIFTIEST
   PAPER AIRPLANE (if you've got
   nothing better to do).
DECAPITATE YOURSELF (and live
   to tell about it).
BE A TWENTY-CARD WIZARD (it
   takes a master manipulator).
CHALLENGE A STRONG MAN (with
   your own muscle, or whatever).

D0040603

SNEAKY FEATS
was originally published by Sheed and Ward, Inc.

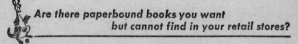

SNEAKY
FEATS

TOM FERRELL
and
LEE EISENBERG

Drawings by Gil Eisner

PUBLISHED BY POCKET BOOKS NEW YORK

SNEAKY FEATS

Sheed and Ward edition published 1975

POCKET BOOK edition published July, 1976

This POCKET BOOK edition includes every word contained in
the original, higher-priced edition. It is printed from brand-
new plates made from completely reset, clear, easy-to-read type.
POCKET BOOK editions are published by
POCKET BOOKS,
a division of Simon & Schuster, Inc.,
A GULF+WESTERN COMPANY
630 Fifth Avenue,
New York, N.Y. 10020.
Trademarks registered in the United States
and other countries.

ISBN: 0-671-80538-X.
Library of Congress Catalog Card Number: 75-1657.

Printed in the U.S.A.

TO OUR MOTHERS
This book is not their fault

CONTENTS

CONTENTS

CONTENTS

INTRODUCTION

Shortly after the creation of man, Cain and Abel, the first two boys on their block, were sitting around with a deck of cards playing War. Cain, for some reason nobody understands, was winning. Abel, who wasn't too swift, but a lot swifter than Cain, suddenly said, "Watch this!" He picked up the deck and cut it a couple of times, using one hand only. Cain tried to appear disinterested. But then Abel placed the deck on his arm and fanned the cards from his elbow to the tips of his fingers. Then, with a mere flick of the hand, Abel flipped the cards over, domino-style.

Cain shifted in his chair as his heart quickened. His reaction was not lost upon Abel. Abel offered the deck to Cain and said in a tone that today, six thousand years later, would be called *condescend-*

ing, "Here. Pick a card. Any card. Don't tell me what it is."

Leaping to his feet, Cain snatched the deck and threw it on the ground. "I hate you!" he cried out. "I hate you for your smugness, your cool superior manner. But most of all I hate you for your skill and for what, six thousand years from now, will be known as *condescension*. You know what you are? You're a show-off!"

Abel sensed that Cain's last taunt was intended to wound him deeply. But why should it? Abel had not only proved his superiority over his brother, he'd found glory in the sight of his Maker, and, most important, in his own. Abel, as is well known, grew up to ace out Cain again and again. Finally, years later, Cain got so fed up he slew Abel in an effort to even the score.

And that, gentle reader, is the story of Abel, the very first show-off, and Cain, the very first chump. Note that from the beginning all the elements of the show-off were fully developed in Abel, to wit:

Competitiveness. The show-off employs certain skills, either innate or acquired, to defeat, humiliate, impress, or simply amuse somebody else, whether a friend, an enemy or a mere stranger. He who shows off, even in a friendly way, is saying, in effect, to the onlooker: "I can do something you can't do. I am better than you." This explains why Cain grew furious at Abel, so much so that he eventually knocked him off. Cain suffered because he couldn't understand how Abel performed his feats. Cain's anguish of soul was only increased by his consciousness that he didn't know any smart (or dumb) tricks. Consequently, Cain got sore. On the other hand, Abel's Creator rejoiced to see Abel's cleverness, hence the familiar saying, "The Lord favors the biggest show-off." And that is as true today as it ever was.

Resourcefulness. More often than not, the show-off is one who realizes, consciously or otherwise, that he has little hope of competing (see above) successfully if he confines his operations to conventional tactics. For an example, observe the recent career of Bobby Riggs. A splendid tennis player in his own day, Riggs came eventually to realize that middle age made it impossible for him to compete against today's best male players. So he decided to play Margaret Court, a woman. Before the match, Riggs showed off by swallowing vast numbers of vitamin pills—and by numerous exhibitions of braggadocio. His antics made his opponent, who probably could have beaten him in a fair match, so nervous that she lost. Later on, Riggs *lost* a match to another woman—an event whose significance we shall explain, but in a paragraph to come. Nevertheless, by playing women rather than men, a tactic many would instantly reject as contemptible, Riggs found instant notoriety (and money). He continues to capitalize, playing regular exhibitions, most of which are marked by one show-off device or another: he'll wear a woman's dress; he'll play while wearing galoshes; he'll take to the side of the court with a number of chairs scattered about. If Riggs were not a show-off, no young American would ever have heard of him. See?

Thirst for glory. Attention is nice, but for a show-off it's not enough. A man who slips on a banana gets *attention* (and laughter), even more so if he breaks his leg. What the show-off is after, above and beyond attention, is *glory.* Someone who shows off is saying to the onlooker, by implication if not out loud, "I have been blessed with wit, imagination, brilliance, or simply an unusual degree of manual dexterity. These things combined, or any one of them, *make me special.*" For a macroscopic example, consider the United States of America. Our country is the mightiest show-off in the world, as its historical mythology reflects: George Washington throwing a dollar across the Rappahannock; Daniel Boone leaving notes around whenever he had kilt a b'ar; Babe Ruth pointing to the place where he intended to hit a home run. The space program of the 1960s was showing off in its purest and most glorious form. To put a man on the moon is to say to the rest of the world: "Look at this! We bet we can put a man on a rocket, shoot him through the black reaches of space, and have him land on his feet on another planet. Ready? Now watch!" And it worked, too. But it might *not* have worked, which brings us to another aspect of the show-off's character. . . .

Courage. The show-off must be competitive and resourceful; when his showing-off succeeds he is consequently glorious as well. But what if he fails? Suppose Washington had thrown the dollar into the soup? Suppose the b'ar had kilt Daniel Boone? Suppose Babe Ruth had popped to the catcher? Showing off is inherently risky. When, for example, the show-off tries to flip a frying egg with one hand and winds up with the egg all over his face, he is laughed at, scorned, put to shame; his bones are licked clean by the onlooking vultures.

If this, of course, were a *perfect* world, people would be more gracious when a show-off embarrassed himself. They would say something like: "Nice form, though, that's for sure. Come on, chin up, try it again. You're tired today, or your wrist hurts, or maybe there was something wrong with the egg." But that's not the world we live in, as the show-off (and everyone else) knows. The world is more like this: "Good! It serves you right! Where does some insecure little twit like you get off trying to impress *me*?! You've made a colossal fool of yourself and I'm glad! Drop dead!" And therefore the show-off, eternally aware of the risk and the consequence of failure, must at all times be courageous. Nothing takes more courage than losing a game nobody asked you to play. And even if you win, there's always the chance you will have beaten some sore loser—like Cain.

Whoever desires the career of a show-off, desires an excellent career, all of the above notwithstanding. But let's face it: *Glory never comes easy.* You win some, you lose some. Fly too close to the sun, or the moon, and you may get burned. Deep in every show-off's heart is this awful knowledge. Holding the pan with the half-fried egg, preparing

to flip it one-handed into space, the show-off says
to himself: "Here goes. If it works, I'm golden. If
it doesn't, I'm cooked. *But it must be done! It's my
only chance! Lord, open Thy gates to me!*" The
show-off can never forget, no matter how he tries,
that for every Charles Lindbergh there's an Amelia
Earhart; for every Neil Armstrong there's an Evel
Knievel; for every Bobby Riggs who plays Margaret
Court, there's a Bobby Riggs who plays Billie Jean
King. Yes, the show-off knows all this; and, knowing it, takes a firmer grip on the skillet and
launches his puny egg into the infinite, toward the
great adventure that is Showing Off.

But we digress. What will you learn from this
book and why should you learn it? At the very
least—assuming you are not totally illiterate or
some kind of perfect gentleman—you will learn
how to perform several dozen feats of the mind
and body. They will come in handy the next time
a party reaches the boring stage, i.e. when nobody
is listening to what you are saying. We might as
well admit it: it's a lot easier to roll a coin across
your knuckles than to actually *think* of something
terrific to *say*. And they will come in handy the
next time somebody is mentally or physically pun-
ishing you. Though showing-off does not assure
victory, it usually causes an opponent to lay off for
a while. Few are versatile enough to punish and
gape at the same time. (But when the novelty
wears off, watch out!)

Sneaky Feats will also teach you a *way of life*,

the Way of the Show-off. It will make you a more confident person, and a more interesting one. It will enable you to convince others that you really *exist*. It will encourage them to remember you, perhaps forever.

The book, you will see, is divided into four parts. "Playing With Your Food" gives you plenty to do when you're at, near, or under a table. "High, Wide and Handy" provides suggestions for everyone with two hands, even if they're both left ones. "Arts and Crafty" features a number of simple items you can make—and to make others fear and respect you. And "So You Want To Be A Stuntman" gives you an assortment of feats to be used wherever and whenever your wicked little heart desires.

—Tom Ferrell
Lee Eisenberg

January 1, 1975
New York City

Part One:

Playing with Your Food

THE ONE-ARMED FRIED EGG

Though it sometimes hurts to admit it, most of a show-off's life is spent eating, sleeping and working, just like ordinary people. We haven't heard of a show-off way to sleep yet, but the subject of eating is endlessly adaptable to those little embroideries and graces that do so much to make life superior. In this respect, the top of the heap is occupied by the world's great chefs, who have spent lifetimes learning how to ignite flaming swords' and the like. But one must start somewhere, and a good place to begin is with the fried egg over easy, using one hand only.

But first, a warning. Do not try to learn one-handed egg-flipping unless you already know how to fry an egg over easy in the orthodox two-handed way. Hot fat and frying pans are not to be trifled with by beginners. But let's assume you can already fry an egg safely and satisfactorily, and go on from there to the show-off's way.

Be sure you have the right kind of frying pan, about seven inches in diameter and light enough —aluminum is best—to handle gracefully with one hand. The pan should have high sides. The best, perhaps, is one of those French models whose sides rise in a gradual curve, but any kind will work as long as the sides are not too low.

Heat some fat in the pan. It's *very important*, now, to use as little fat as you can, because you do *not* want to be splashed with hot fat when you reach the flipping stage. The modern non-stick Teflon-surfaced frying pan allows you to use the least fat. When the fat has reached frying heat, you are ready to proceed with the first fancy step, as shown on the opposite page.

Break the egg with one hand only. To do this, grasp the egg as shown in figure 1 and give it a determined, but not violent, crack on the side of the pan or any other hard surface. The idea is to produce a fracture running all the way around the egg, without penetrating the yolk. Very swiftly open the egg as shown in figure 2, letting the gooey inside of the egg drop into the pan. It may help you through this step to handle the egg as though it had a hinge at the top between the two halves of the shell. Sometimes, no matter how deft you are, this step fails and all you get is a handful of

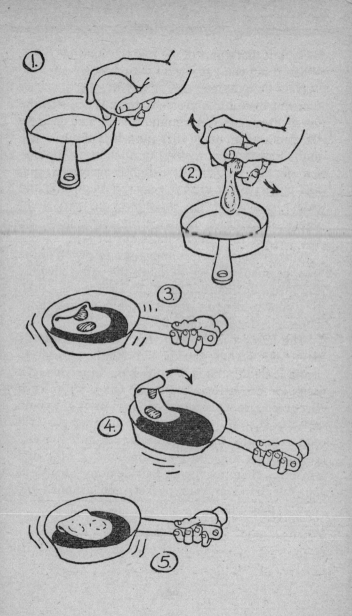

mess, but that's part of the risk the show-off takes. When it happens, try again with another egg.

Now that the egg is in the pan, just let it sit there a while until one side is done. When only the top of the egg is still wet and uncoagulated, jiggle the pan a bit to make sure the whole thing is free and slides around, instead of sticking to the bottom. Pick up the pan, tilt it slightly away from you, and jiggle the pan until the egg slides downhill and begins to slide up the far side of the pan, as in figure 3. Continue to jiggle and slide until the egg reaches the critical stage (figure 4).

Then, with a short, snappy upward twitch of the pan, persuade the egg to follow the path shown by the arrow in figure 4, until it assumes the position shown in figure 5. Cook the other side until done, and there you have it.

The hardest part about the whole procedure is doing everything quickly but gently enough to avoid breaking the yolk during the flip, when the egg is in the half-cooked stage. One way to learn the procedure without risk is to fry an egg on both sides in the ordinary way, then use the pre-fried egg to practice figures 3 through 5 until you can perform the flip with a minimum of risk and violence. Then invite your friends in for breakfast, put one hand in your pocket, and astonish the world's morning.

SLICING A BANANA
WITHOUT PEELING IT

Even the humble banana is useful for showing off. Suppose you give your best friend a banana. He will be surprised, no doubt, but only mildly so. However, imagine his astonishment when he peels the banana and finds that, within the apparently unbroken skin, the banana is already sliced! Before his eyes the whole thing will fall into neat segments as he peels it.

To peel a banana inside its skin, follow these steps:

1) Take a fully-ripe banana and a fine needle, long enough to reach from one side of the banana to the other, threaded with about two feet of fine silk or synthetic thread. Do not use a young, fresh, waxy-looking all-yellow unblemished banana, for it is actually necessary to pierce the skin many

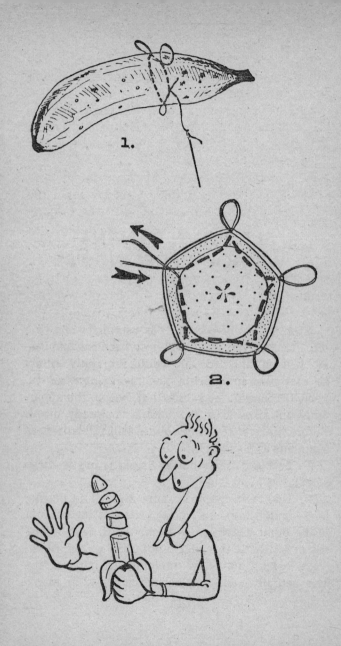

1.

2.

times, and you don't want the holes to show. The dull and partially blackened skin of a ripe banana helps conceal the holes.

2) Pierce the banana anywhere along its length, inserting the needle at one of the banana's corners (a banana is not cylindrical, but more like a five-sided prism). Pass the needle under the skin of the banana to the next corner. Draw the needle and most of the thread out, but be sure to leave the end of the thread protruding from the original entry point.

3) Insert the needle back into the hole just made in the second corner, and proceed to draw it out through the third corner, and so on until the needle and thread emerge from the original point of entry. A cross-section of the banana at the working site now looks like the drawing.

4) Take both ends of the thread and pull. As the thread is withdrawn through the original entry hole, the flesh of the banana will be sliced through.

Repeat the entire process at different sites along the banana until you have made as many slices as you wish. The banana is now sliced inside its skin. The holes will not be noticeable except on very close inspection. And who is going to look that closely at a banana?

THE SEVEN-LAYER
POUSSE-CAFE (HOO-HAH!)

The next time you have important guests over to the house, be a big shot after dinner by making a seven-layer pousse-cafe. Start showing off by pronouncing it right (pooskafay) and explaining that it means coffee-pusher in French. To make it, take seven after-dinner liqueurs of contrasting colors and different specific gravities (specific gravity, which depends on the proportions of water, sugar and alcohol in the beverages, may be determined with a hydrometer from a dealer in laboratory supplies; or a wine-maker's saccharometer will do the job).

Line up the bottles with the heaviest liqueur first and the lightest, which is usually cognac, at the end. For this example we choose: (1) white anisette; (2) creme de cacao; (3) white creme de menthe; (4) apricot liqueur; (5) triple sec; (6) Chartreuse; (7) cognac.

Now, pour a quantity of the heaviest liqueur—in this case, the white anisette—into a spoon and dribble it down the side of a tall, thin liqueur glass. Actually, since this is the bottom layer, it is OK to just slop it in.

Take a like quantity of liqueur number two, the second heaviest, and dribble it slowly from the spoon down the side of the glass, so that it does not mix with the liqueur below but floats on it, spreading out into a layer of contrasting color (figure 1, page 30).

Repeat the process, being careful not to disturb the glass, until all seven liqueurs are neatly arranged in layers (figure 2). There you have it.

There's more than one way to show off when you drink your seven-layer pousse-cafe. You may sip the product from top to bottom; or, using a long, fine straw, from bottom to top.

Or, instead of making it at home, you may order one in a bar. If the bartender doesn't know how to make it, insist on demonstrating to him. Then, when the whole thing is made with all the layers perfectly arranged after a lot of time and trouble and irritation, just knock the whole thing back in one great gulp!

1.

2.

COGNAC
MERINGUE
ICE CREAM
COOKIE PAPER
WOODEN BLOCK

VOILA!
FLAMING BAKED ALASKA!

Showing off at the dinner table begins early in life—with throwing peas, or eating them from a knife. Advanced showing off, however, requires time, preparation, thought, and the sincere desire to astonish. One way is to present guests or members of the family with something to eat that's a real gasper—an irresistible center of attraction and admiration.

Such an object is the Flaming Baked Alaska, or *omelette norvegienne*, which has a wholly exaggerated reputation for difficulty. You, of course, can profit by the reputation; it's best not to make this where people can find out how easy it really is. The following récipe gives you a small product, just right for two people; for a bigger one, use a slice of sponge cake, or a sheet of sugar-cookie dough baked in a slab, for a base, and increase other proportions accordingly.

1. Separate three eggs, dropping the whites in the Mixmaster bowl. If you are unable to keep other people out of the kitchen, impress them now by swallowing the yolks whole; otherwise, throw them away. Add about a third of a cup of sugar

and a pinch of cream of tartar to the egg whites. Then beat like crazy until the meringue is stiff enough that it stands up in little peaks when you withdraw the mixer blades.

2. Take a round half-pint carton of ice cream (peach or strawberry is nice) and a big, thick, hard cookie—Chinese almond cookies are good—about the same size as the big end of the ice-cream carton. The ice cream should be firm but not rock-hard.

Cut a piece of brown paper about an inch bigger than the cookie. Put the paper on a wooden cutting board or similar slab—do not use a metal pan. Put the cookie in the middle of the paper, get the ice cream out of the carton in one piece and put it on the cookie. Slather the meringue all over, sealing carefully—but hurry.

3. Slide the whole thing into the oven, which you have carefully preheated to 500 degrees. Inspect after about two minutes, then keep checking at one-minute intervals. When the meringue is brown in patches on the outside, it's done. This won't take more than five minutes altogether, so don't forget to keep an eye on it.

4. Pick up the Baked Alaska with a pancake turner and slide it onto a plate, getting rid of the paper if you can. Now, take about an ounce of cognac or a fruit-flavored liqueur such as curaçao, which you have carefully warmed by putting it in a small glass, covering the glass with aluminum foil, and standing it for a few minutes in a pan of hot water (you must warm it because it will

not ignite at room temperature). Pour it into the smallest saucepan you have (but one with a long handle) and touch a match to it. (WHOOSH!) Pour it instantly over the Baked Alaska. (SIZZLE!) Be sure the dish you put the Baked Alaska on is big enough so that none of the flaming liqueur will run over the sides onto the table. Present it immediately, before the fire goes out. Make a wish and fall to.

HOW TO CLEAN A FISH

What do we like to do to relax after hours of wowing friends and strangers with mind-boggling tricks? We like to go down to the lake and fish. It isn't actually hard to catch fish—beginners are often as successful as old-timers—so this feat won't provide any flashy tips on angling. Rather, it will help you in the après-catch department, that is, how to clean a fish after you've caught him.

You'll be glad for these tips when you and your partners are standing around muttering, "Yech! Now who is going to touch those icky things and turn them into a tasty meal?" Here's how you can step forward and take control on the spot:

Wash your fish in cold water. Make sure your fish is dead, then place him on the ground. If your fish has fins, cut them off before scaling. A fin can give you an annoying nick. If the fish has scales, take a knife or fish-scaler (there's a dandy from Sweden that sells for around four bucks) and, holding the fish at the tail, scrape carefully forward toward the head (figure 1). You can easily see the scales come off; run your thumb along the fish to feel for any that remain.

Now comes the disgusting part. Like everyone else, fish have gicky stuff inside them. Your job is to get it all out. Using a sharp knife, make a slit up the bottom of the fish, beginning just above the tail and ending right below the head (figure 2). You want to remove the entrails. Once the fish is slit, you'll see them, honest. They come out easily—simply take your knife or hand and flip them out. Make sure to get all of it (gulp).

Chances are, if you're cleaning fish for the first time, you won't want to keep looking at the head anymore. No problem! Take your knife and, your eye and stomach as steady as a brain surgeon's, remove it. It doesn't hurt the fish at all, and it will only make you queasy for a few minutes. Now do the same to the tail, which is a lot easier. Here now is your fish ready for frying or broiling (figure 3). It looks totally innocent, doesn't it?

Please be very careful when cleaning fish. Use a sharp knife and always hold the fish firmly. The worst thing in the world is for a show-off to wear a band-aid. It's humiliating, to say the least.

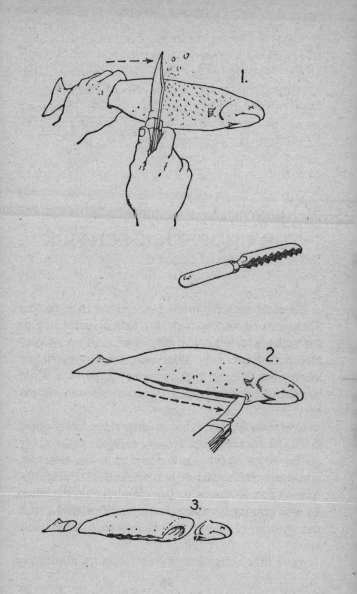

THE CHOPSTICK SCHTICK

There is nothing more inscrutable than eating Chinese food with a fork. It's ridiculously easy to eat with chopsticks—hundreds of millions of people do it every day. Most round-eyed Americans know how to do it, too, but every once in a while you run across a poor chap like the one shown here.

Everyone at the table is throwing down chow mein effortlessly; this fellow, though, picks away at the slippery fare, rice falling on his trousers, lain-drops falling from his head. But as unfortunate as this situation is, imagine his chagrin when he sees you manipulate the mysterious sticks with the wisdom of Confucius. Here's how in two easy steps:

Your first obligation is to establish a stationary

stick. Hold it in the crotch of your thumb, as in figure 1, and with the ring finger of that hand. Balance the stick at the most comfortable point.

Your second obligation is to establish a movable stick, as in figure 2. Use the tip of your thumb and the second and third fingers. Now make like Groucho Marx (but don't move your eyebrows, the Chinese didn't find him funny). Pick up your delicious food with the ends of the sticks and shovel it into your mouth. You don't need us to tell you how to do that. Or do you?

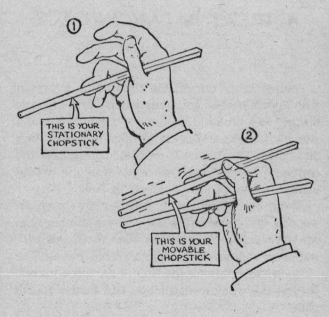

THIS IS YOUR STATIONARY CHOPSTICK

THIS IS YOUR MOVABLE CHOPSTICK

A GREAT BALANCING ACT

Among other things, the show-off is a person who knows how to get along when the going gets boring. Say you're at a dinner party and you and the others have told every terrifically funny story you know. The dessert is an upside-down flop, the coffee tastes like sludge, and everyone would rather be home eating crackers in bed.

There are a number of ways to save such an evening and here we'll show you yet another one. All you need are four glasses filled two-thirds with water, as well as three ordinary table knives. The mission: to interlock the knives on three glasses so that the whole construction can hold a fourth glass.

Dare the guests to effect this, telling them they must arrange the knives in triangular fashion, handles on each glass, blades touching at the center.

There are really only a few things you need to know to achieve what this sneaky guy in the drawing on page 42 is achieving. It comes down to how you interlock the knives. The insert shows all: Knife 1 goes over 2 and under 3. Knife 2 goes over 3 and under 1. Knife 3 goes over 1 and under 2.

This interlocking system should be placed upon the glasses on the sides of the rims facing the center of the construction. Do not balance the knives on both sides of the rim of the glass; this makes the feat look easy. If you do all this correctly, the fourth glass will stand triumphantly on the knives.

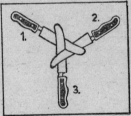

THE ALL-WET, INSULTING TIP

The revenge of a show-off can be terrible. Suppose you have stopped off at some roadside hash-house for a cup of coffee and a piece of pie, and you've been disappointed with the pie, the coffee, and the service, not to mention the greasy smells and high prices. How do you get even? By leaving a nickel tip underneath an inverted glass of water is how. This easily-accomplished stunt takes advantage of the well-known fact that atmospheric pressure at sea level is something like fifteen pounds per square inch (less in Colorado, but still enough to work) and therefore will support a column of water.

To do it, take a very full glass of water (if your glass isn't full enough, borrow another and fill yours right up to the brim). Drop the nickel in

1.

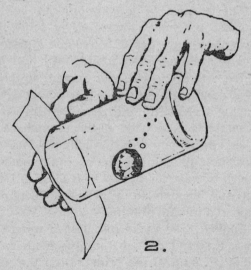

2.

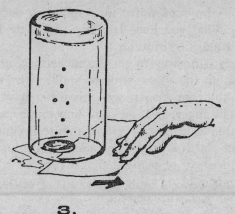

3.

(see figure 1). Then take a fairly stiff piece of paper of a convenient size and put it over the mouth of the glass.

Now, holding the paper lightly but firmly in place, invert the glass (figure 2). When the glass is upside down remove your hand. The paper—and the water above it, and the nickel—will stay in place. But don't dawdle, because the paper will soak through pretty soon and the whole thing will fall apart.

Set the inverted glass on the counter or table. The top of the counter or table must be Formica or some similar smooth surface; this won't work on a tablecloth, which is why we're teaching it to you in a hash-house. But then if you were in a fancy restaurant with a tablecloth you probably wouldn't be mad enough to be pulling this trick. Now slide the paper out from under the glass (figure 3). Two or three drops of water may spill out, but don't worry. What you have left is a nickel tip inside an inverted glass of water.

There is no way to get the nickel out, or even to pick up the glass, without spilling the water. When the counterman sees what you have done he will be angry, and you know how tough counter-men are, so learn to perform this technique fast and get out in a hurry. For additional injury and insult, instead of using a nickel drop in a small foreign coin of no value whatsoever; Austrian ten-groschen pieces are perfect.

Part Two:

High, Wide and Handy

THE GRAND
RUBBER BAND MYSTERY

Long ago, everybody lived on farms, and the handiest way to show off was by walking up and down in front of the house on top of the picket fence. Nowadays, of course, nobody lives on farms any more; everybody lives in offices. Picket fences everywhere have been replaced by wire mesh, which is just about impossible to walk on top of; but offices are full of dandy furniture for showing off with.

Take, for example, the humble rubber band. (Of course if you do still live on a farm, or even in an ordinary house, you should still be able to find some kind of rubber band.) Anyhow, your object is, first, to wrap the rubber band inextricably around the fingers; second, to extricate the whole mess in a dazzling flash that nobody can understand. In fact, though we can show you how to do it, we don't profess to understand it ourselves. Just follow the directions, bearing in mind that all the illustrations are shown from your own point of view, not that of an observer.

Stick out your index finger (we show the left index finger, because it's easier for most people to use the right hand to work on the left) and hang a rubber band on it (figure 1).

Grab the rubber band with your right hand and rotate it one-half turn to the right, as shown in figure 2.

Draw the rubber band—both halves of it—with your right hand away and below under your middle finger and wrap it round your index finger again, exactly as shown in figure 3. It's easy to go wrong here, but there's only one way to go wrong, so follow the drawing carefully, and if when you get to the end this doesn't work, go back and do it the other way. When you've finished the wrapping, the whole business should look like figure 4.

Now comes the dazzling flash. Close your thumb on the tip of your index finger. Obviously there is now no way in the world to get the rubber band off your hand. However, you have only to wiggle your middle finger for a bit and zowie, the rubber band flies free (figure 5). Don't ask us why. Sometimes the rubber band will hang up on the middle finger, but if snapped briskly and with a perky enough band it will fly halfway across the room.

Don't ask us how, either. Just rejoice that nobody else will ever be able to figure it out, no matter how many times you repeat it. It drives them crazy, and that's where the show-off wants them to be.

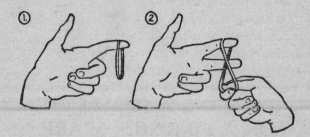

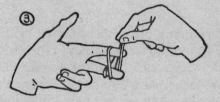

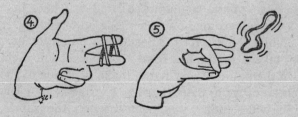

SNUFFING A CIGARETTE
ON A FINE SILK SCARF

There are many places to show off with this trick. We suggest you sit in a fancy French restaurant and wait for a rich beautiful woman to walk by. If you're lucky, she'll drop her St. Laurent scarf at your feet. Reach down and pick it up, stub out your cigarette on it, then hand it back with a smile. The ice has been broken and you've impressed the heck out of the woman. We'll tell you here how it's done; learning how to smile is up to you.

While waiting for the beautiful woman to show up, take a half-dollar from your pocket and hold it in the palm of your hand. Make sure it is in the center of your palm (figure 1, page 54). (The coin will conduct the heat through the fabric, leaving the fabric undamaged.)

Now the woman walks by and drops the scarf.

Pick it up with your free hand and wave it in the air with a flourish. This will make her realize there are no cigarette burns on the scarf to begin with. It will also remove attention from the hand holding the coin. Transfer the scarf to the hand with the coin. Open your fingers and place the scarf over your palm (figure 2).

If the coin should slip out of your hand, abandon everything; you could wind up burning yourself. Just hand the scarf back, remembering not to blush. If all goes well, however, flick the loose ashes off the cigarette. A clean butt is of utmost importance; lingering bits of fire will burn holes. Now stub out the cigarette on the coin in three or four confident taps (figure 3).

Before you hand back the scarf, whisk it off the hand with the coin and shake it briskly. This will remove any remaining ashes from the scarf. The scarf has suffered no damage. If, though, you missed the coin and burned the scarf, offer to pay for it. A show-off is never a cheapskate.

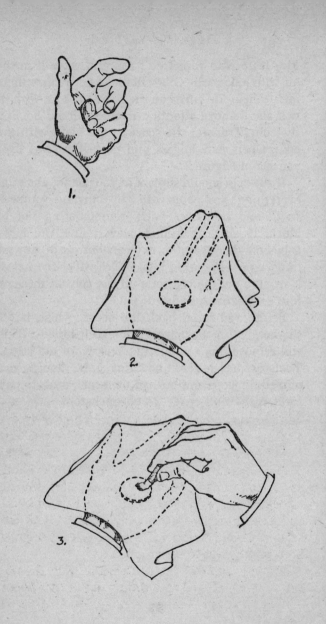

CUTTING THE DECK
WITH ONE HAND

If you like movies such as "The Sting," you'll love knowing how to cut the deck with one hand. You're sitting at the table with some sharpie on your right, a fellow who blows perfect smoke rings from a long, thin cheroot. He places the deck before you with disdain. You pause, then slowly extend your hand and pick it up. Bam! Bam! You slice the fifty-two with one hand—and not while the deck is still resting on the table. Want to know how to pull this off? Well, as promised, here's how:

Pick up the deck with your most trusted hand and turn it over, as shown in figure 1. Hold the deck with your thumb and the tips of your fingers. Keep your fingers fairly straight.

Holding the deck in place with your thumb, move the knuckle of your thumb out so that about half the cards drop down to your palm (figure 2). Before going further, practice this move until you can do it smoothly.

With the tip of your index finger, push the bottom half of the deck up toward your thumb (figure 3). Imagine that the cards are hinged at the heel of your hand—this will enable you to go only as far as you must. Open your hand slightly and, while holding the bottom half of the deck between your index finger and thumb, let the top half slide down over your index finger (figure 4). Now all you have to do is close your thumb and you will have the full cut deck, as well as a psychological edge on your opponents.

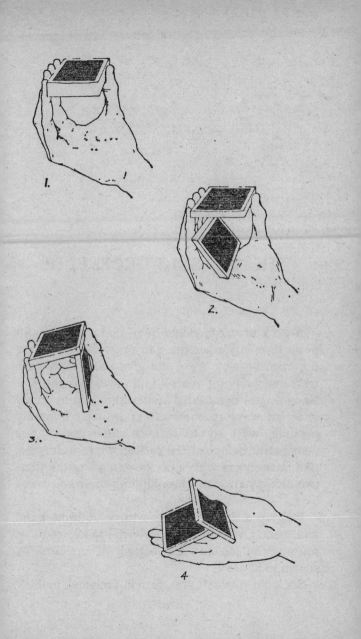

1.

2.

3.

4

THE CLASSIC DECK FLIP

A deck of cards yields more hours of fun and profit than any other thing in the world, including the opposite sex. We could give you a new card trick every day for years—and never run out. But since we are committed to teaching you as many different ways to show off as is super-humanly possible, we'll try to restrain ourselves to just demonstrating one of the easiest, yet most impressive, maneuvers with a deck—spreading the fifty-two along your arm, then flipping the whole mess over.

Pick up a deck of cards with your right hand and, gently, so you don't blow the whole routine, squeeze the top and the bottom of the deck as shown in figure 1.

Stick out your left arm, firm but relaxed, making

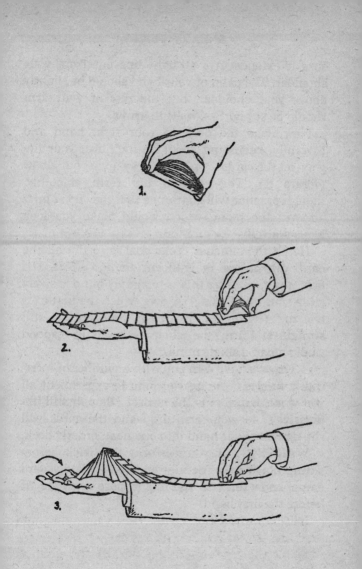

sure it extends in a straight line out from your shoulder. The palm of your hand should be slightly above your shoulder, but the rest of your arm should be straight as, well, an arrow.

Now, take the deck in your right hand and carefully, beginning about an inch over your fingers, let the cards drop all the way up to your elbow (figure 2). They should flip forth smoothly, though practice will guarantee that they don't buzz all over the room, which would make you look like a real silly.

Here's the clincher. Your goal is to flip all the cards over in one magnificent domino effect. The best way to achieve this is to simply but decisively close your middle fingers, over which the first card is lying (figure 3). Do it! If your arm is still straight and firm, the whole deck should respond as though of a single mind.

Experts have come up with a number of interesting finales. You are welcome to experiment all you want, but here is the easiest (though still impressive): let your arm drop and the cards will slip down to your hand into one neat, orderly deck.

WARNING: If you perform this trick before sitting down to a friendly or not-so-friendly card game, know full well you might scare everyone off before the first hand.

POP GOES THE BRACELET

This little manipulative technique drives people crazy to watch, but even crazier if they try it themselves. And they will try it themselves, because, unlike true tricks of sleight-of-hand, it is all done in the open and looks easy. Even if you have the ability to palm coins and make cigarettes disappear into thin air, you'll find it difficult to make people try to imitate your performance because they know they can't; whereas the bracelet pop conceals nothing, and therefore attracts the suckers to attempt to do likewise. Nothing establishes the superiority of the show-off faster.

All you need for the bracelet pop is two hands and a bracelet. The bracelet should be made of some plastic or metal that won't break when dropped, because dropping it in a spectacular way is what you intend to do. Don't try it with a wrist watch. In fact, the bracelet pop should only be performed over a table or similar surface to stop the fall. Here's how, now (please note that figures 1 through 4 are drawn from the point-of-view of the performer):

1. Loop the bracelet over your forefingers and rotate it for a while by twirling your fingers in the direction shown in figure 1. If you find twirling in this direction awkward, twirl in the opposite direction; it doesn't make the slightest difference.

2. Stop twirling when your right hand is low and your left high, as shown in figure 2, and close the fingers and thumbs of your hands firmly on each other around the bracelet. The bracelet itself should remain loose; be sure not to pinch it.

3. Bring your hands together as shown in figure 3, with the thumbs and forefingers all touching in the center of the bracelet. Notice, however, that the tip of the right forefinger is adjacent to and touching the tip of the left thumb, and the tip of the left forefinger makes contact with the tip of the right thumb. Got it?

4. Open your hands exactly as shown in figure 4, with the tips of the opposite forefingers and thumbs firmly pressed together. The bracelet falls free. What's so amazing about that, you ask. Well, the answer is that the faster and more gracefully you do it the more amazing it becomes, because, to all appearances, the bracelet passes right through, not between, your fingers. Where, after all, did you let go? You appear to have had a firm

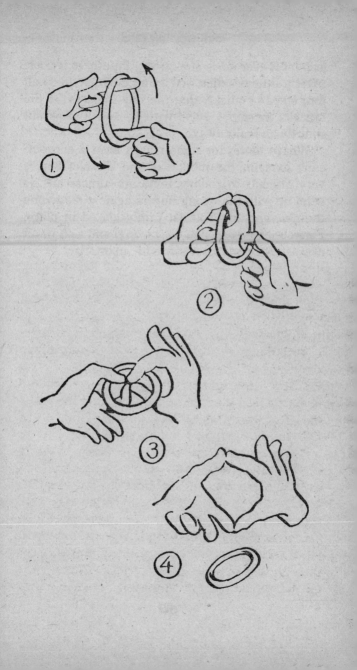

grip on it ever since step 2, yet, flip! there it goes. After a little practice, you'll find it simple to do all four steps so quickly that the spin imparted to the bracelet in step 1 stays with it, and it pops out smartly and rolls away.

What's more, for some reason even a show-off can't explain, the motion of the bracelet pop is very difficult to follow; imitators almost always wind up with the wrong fingers against the wrong thumbs, and the bracelet firmly locked in place. For you it works, for them it won't; and a show-off can ask for no greater sense of superiority.

THE RING AND THE STRING

The virtue of this little beauty lies in its use of everyday materials to produce an effect totally beyond the comprehension of the observer. In fact, we're not so sure we comprehend it ourselves, but we're going to show you how it's done all the same; then you can figure it out at leisure. What happens is, you thread a loop of string through the middle of a ring (or anything else with a hole in it) and ask someone to hold the string on his fingers (figure 1). Then, by a few deft manipulations, you remove the ring from the string, without ever lifting the string off the fingers! Obviously this is impossible, so don't trouble your mind about trying to figure it out; show-offs have more important things to think about. Just follow the instructions and take the credit. Here's how:

65

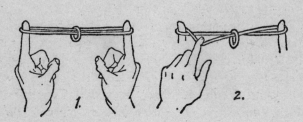

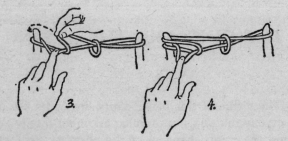

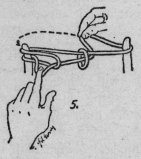

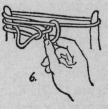

Leaving the ring in about the middle of the strings, reach over the near string with the left hand, grasp the far string, and pull it toward you over the top of the near string (figure 2).

Now, with your right hand, reach underneath the string you are holding in your left hand. Grab the remaining string—the one you are not holding in your left hand—a little to the right of the left hand, and pull the string toward you. Pull out some slack, and loop it once around your victim's right index finger (left from your point of view) (figure 3), and let go with the right hand, but keep holding on to the string in your left (figure 4).

Next, with your right hand reach over the near string on the right side of the ring, grab the far string, and pull it into another loop over the right (left, as we said, from your point of view) index finger of the patsy (figure 5). Don't let go with the left hand yet! And don't worry about where the ring has slid to by now.

Finally, grab the ring with your right hand. Let go of the string in your left hand. Pull gently on the ring (figure 6). The strings will all slide around a little bit and the ring will be free. If you don't believe us, just try it.

Now you know the fundamentals; variations are up to your ingenuity. Gilt string from Christmas wrappings makes the whole trick particularly tasteful; or if your style of showing off calls for gigantism, you might want to use a big piece of rope and a bicycle tire.

THE PEARL OF INDIA
AFFINITY TEST

You are having lunch or dinner with a beautiful lady. You tell her that by virtue of your mystic powers you can determine whether she is your true soul-mate. If she's still listening, you invite her to participate in an ancient mystic rite of India. It is, of course, quite decent. What you need, you say, is a priceless pearl and a beaker of acid, but since you are having lunch, a cube of sugar and a glass of water will do. You hand the beautiful creature the cube of sugar, and invite her to draw on it, with a pen, a clear and simple design—say, a heart with your initial on it. You take the cube of sugar, flourish it, and drop it into a glass of water, or a cup of coffee. The cube of sugar is now gone, destroyed, right? Right. Now, for the grand finale and most impressive effect ever, you invite her to concentrate for a few seconds on the palms of her hands; then to hold her hands directly over the glass of water and concentrate a few seconds longer. Then you say: "Turn your hands over." And there, big as life, on one palm, is the exact design she drew on the cube of sugar! And yet the cube, which she never touched, is under water dissolving. She is yours!

Now, how is this done? Let's go back to the design on the sugar (figure 1, page 70). This must be clear, simple and in ink. If it's not clear and simple enough, tell her the spirits don't like it and ask for another.

When the spirits are satisfied, pick up a glass of ice water with your left hand and move it to the center of the table. The ostensible purpose of this move is ceremonial; the real purpose is to dampen your thumb slightly from the condensation on the outside of the glass. Then, when you pick up the sugar cube and say the magic word *mekkamussulmannenmonumentenmacher*, the design will be transferred to your damp and slightly sticky thumb —provided, of course, you have your thumb square on the design (figure 2). The rest is child's play; when she holds her hands over the glass with the sugar, help her adjust their position. Press the palm of her hand, which of course is facing down over the glass, just once with your thumb (figure 3). Don't smear! The design is now transferred. Now it's up to you to get your thumb out of the way without being spotted, carry on with the hocus-pocus for a few more seconds, and ask her to turn over. Perfect! Now just don't forget *mekka-mussulmannenmonumentenmacher*, but if you forget it anyhow, try *abracadabra*.

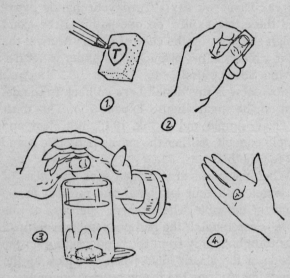

WHISTLING THROUGH GRASS

Going out into the fields and meadows is supposed to be relaxing, but the true show-off never misses an opportunity. A classic pastoral attention-grabber is whistling through a blade of grass. Many of you probably know how to do this, while more of you have doubtless seen and heard it performed. For those of you who have somehow missed the boat, here's all there is to it.

But first, *when* do you whistle through grass? Our opinion is that you wait until it's very quiet, when the only sounds you hear are the sweet chirping of crickets and the melodic strains of birds in the trees. Then you pluck a blade, place it between your hands, and blow. The crickets and birds will fall at your feet, deeply in awe.

Pick a blade of grass around six inches long.

Hold it between your thumb and index finger. With your other hand, pull the blade tight against the thumb holding it (figure 1).

Keep the edge of the blade facing you. The point is to have as narrow a surface as possible close to your mouth. The best position is shown in figure 2.

Place your left thumb against your right thumb. Your hands come together in two places: at the thumbs' first knuckles and at the ball of the hand below each thumb. Make sure to lock the blade in at these two points; keep the blade as rigid as possible (figure 3).

Now blow steadily, not too strong, not too weak. Practice until you get a smooth, confident sound. Once you master this trick you'll never forget it. It's like swimming and riding a bicycle.

There are a number of other great stunts you can pull off in the woods. But don't expect us to teach you these. This, remember, is family entertainment.

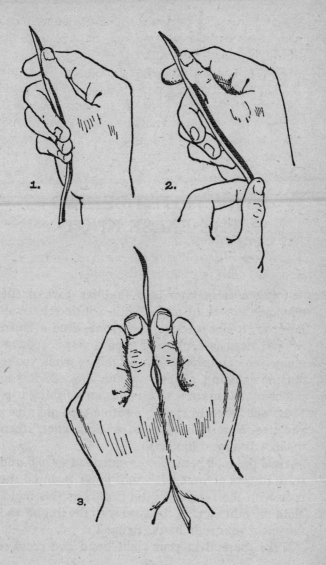

THE TRUTH BEHIND
THE FALSE KNOT

Tying a false knot is a familiar part of the magician's stock in trade. With a little rehearsal, however, it can be done by anyone, even a klutz. All you need is a piece of rope a few feet long. Mom, you can impress the neighbors when you're outside hanging clothes on the line. Dad, you might try to amaze your buddies on a fishing trip. Kids, well, you can show off with a rope anywhere you like. Here is how to tie a "tight knot," then make it disappear in a flash.

Hold the rope between the extended second and third fingers of your left hand; press down on the rope with the ring and little fingers of this hand. Hold the other end of the rope with the thumb and fingers of your right hand (figure 1).

Take the end in your right hand and cross it

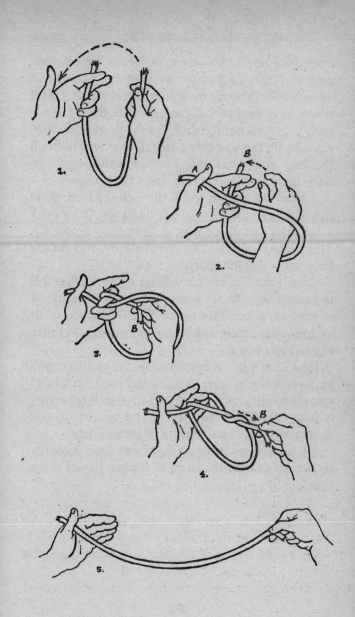

over your left hand—over the point where your ring and little fingers are holding down their end of the rope. Droop it over your left hand and let it rest next to your thumb (point A in figure 2). Now, with your free hand, reach for the end of the rope marked B. You are going to pull this end through the loop you've created, but not until you introduce the sneaky little maneuver that follows.

As you are pulling end B through the loop, bend the middle finger of your left hand and draw back a little loop in the opposite direction (figure 3). This second loop is a slip knot; without it, your big knot will not come apart.

Once your slip knot has been made, pull end B to form a tight knot (figure 4). But be careful not to yank on it too hard or too fast. What you want to do is stop before the knot comes apart. Practice will tell you when.

Now here's the punch line. You may either pull both ends of the rope to make the knot vanish, or you may run your hand across the rope, removing it that way. Try it both ways and see which one gives you the greater feeling of importance.

All this seems more complicated than it really is. You should get the hang of it after two or three tries.

AN OLD SWITCHEROO

Showing off can be divided into two main kinds of behavior. The first consists of doing things that are spectacular in themselves, like riding a bicycle "no-hands." The second is made up of doing things that nobody else can do, no matter how dumb the things are in themselves, like, for instance, card tricks. There isn't any earthly reason for card tricks, but that doesn't stop audiences from gaping enthusiastically at the simplest sleights. Likewise, the only reason for learning the Old Switcheroo is because once you know it, you'll find that nobody else can figure it out.

Here's what you do: you pick up a couple of small cylindrical objects in the forks of your thumbs, as shown in figure 1. Corks are good, and so are lipsticks or 35-millimeter film cans.

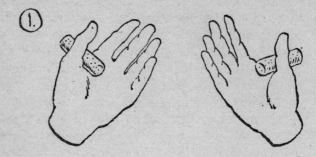

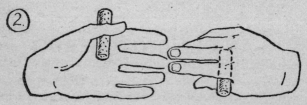

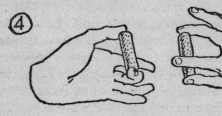

Then, holding one in each hand, you proceed to do the following impossible thing. Grasp the left-hand cork, or whatever you are using, between the thumb and fingers of your right hand. At the same time, grasp the right-hand cork between the thumb and fingers of your left hand. Finally, with a twist of the wrist, separate the hands without letting go of the corks. Does that sound easy? If it does, just try it at this point without reading the rest of the instructions.

To do it right, go back to figure 1. Now, rotate your right hand palm-down, as shown in figure 2.

Now, bring your hands together (figure 3), with the right hand above the left. Keep the two corks parallel to each other. Grasp the corks exactly as shown. Apparently the fingers and corks are inextricably tangled-up together, and that's the beauty of the trick; in actual fact they aren't interlocked at all, as we shall presently see.

Now, you can simply draw your hands apart, as shown in figure 4. But it's much more impressive to give a little twist of the wrists before doing so, because a half-turn or so obscures the action and gives the illusion that the corks have passed right through each other.

Keep repeating this action until you can do it smoothly and swiftly. Then go out and challenge someone you know to do the same. Unless you deliberately explain step-by-step, you'll have him sweating and straining and red with rage as he cobbles up his fingers something awful trying to solve it.

MASTERING
THE FRENCH DROP

This is a splendidly versatile trick of magic that will serve you until death. You've seen it a zillion times; some people use coins, others ping-pong balls. As long as an object fits neatly into your palm, it's a good drop prop. The trick is this: you make something disappear into thin air, then reproduce it. It's easy to do but not so easy for an audience to figure out.

Hold a coin, say a quarter, between the thumb and index finger of your left hand. Use the tips of these two fingers exclusively, as in figure 1.

Slowly pass the thumb of your right hand under the coin in a smooth, even motion, as in figure 2.

You want to give the impression that this right hand is actually taking the coin. But instead of transferring the coin, you let it drop from the

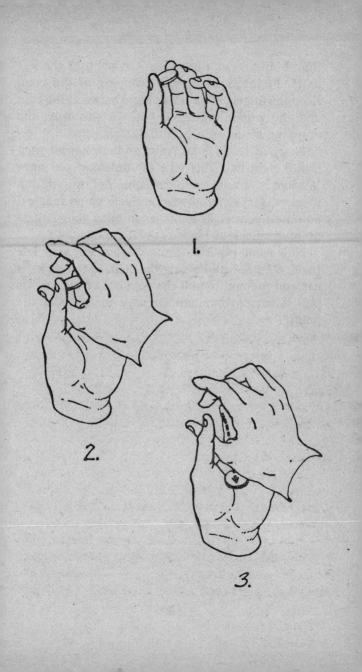

1.

2.

3.

thumb and index finger into the palm of the left hand. Figure 3 shows the dropping of the coin. Keep the fingers of your left hand between the coin and the person watching you. In this way, the dropping of the coin is entirely concealed.

Now, to really hook your audience, present a closed right fist. This tells the onlooker you have "obviously" transferred the coin. Ask the chump to blow, tap, or otherwise activate some magical power on your right hand. Then open your fingers dramatically. Huh? Where did it go?

Now some possible grand finales. Put your left hand, the one still holding the coin, to the sucker's ear and pretend to pull the coin out of his ear. Or pull it out of your ear. Or your mouth. Get the point?

FOUR IMPRESSIVE
SHADOW PICTURES

Anybody can deface a wall with spray paint, but while the graffiti artist may think he's a big shot, he's really just a cheap shot. When you're faced with a nice clean wall and nothing to do, don't be dumb and destructive, be classy and creative.

Shadow pictures are easily learned and very impressive. All you need is a source of concentrated light and a white wall or screen. One of the best light sources is a slide or movie projector. Try showing off with shadow pictures after you've shown shots of your last vacation and bored everybody silly. Here are four terrific designs with which to start your repertoire. After you've mastered them, try coming up with some of your own (fat chance, right?).

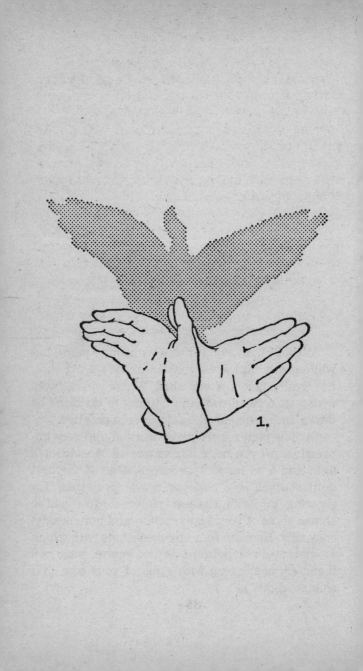

1.

Figure 1—The Flying Dove

This is one of the basic designs. To get the dove moving, flap your fingers gracefully.

Figure 2—The Black Rabbit

There are three moving parts here: wiggle your top fingers to make his ears twitch; move the middle, ring, and little fingers of your bottom hand to get him sniffing and chomping; close your hand slightly to make him blink.

Figure 3—Mother Goose

You'll have to roll up your sleeves for this (unless you want your goose to look like she's wearing a collar). Close your ring and little fingers to get her squawking.

Figure 4—Mr. Tortoise

This one's a bit tougher to master, but keep trying. You can make his head sway and go into his shell. But are you smart enough to figure out how?

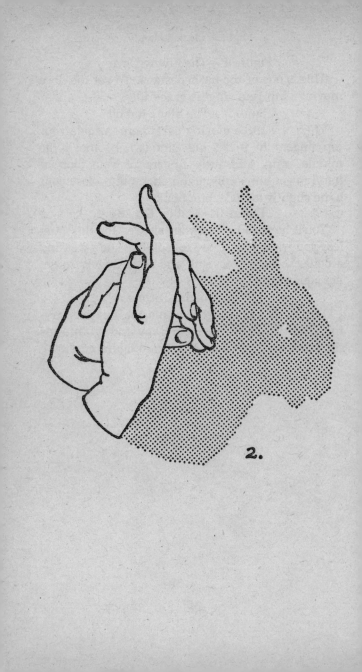

2.

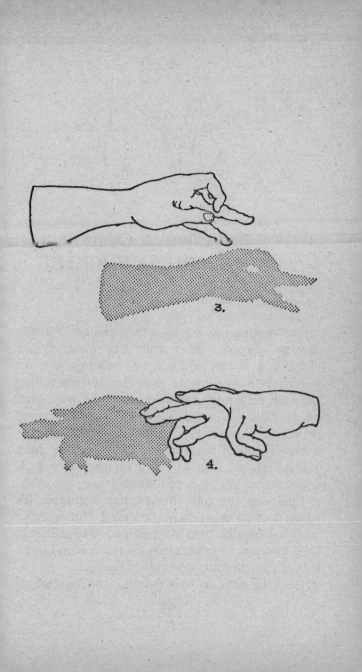

3.

4.

ROLLING A COIN
ACROSS YOUR KNUCKLES

You've seen this beauty a hundred times in the movies: a cowboy in a white hat stands by the corral just as cool and tough as can be. He takes out a coin, smiles a little, then stands there rolling the coin across his knuckles, first one way, then back again. You can do it while waiting to buy popcorn at the movies, or on the corner waiting for a bus. It will make you feel like a young John Wayne. Here's how to roll a quarter or a half-dollar across the top of your knuckles.

Don't use any coin smaller than a quarter, it's rough doing with a penny or a nickel. Moisten your middle knuckles with your tongue; this will help keep the coin from slipping. Place the coin on the side of your thumb, as shown in figure 1.

Hold the coin on your thumb until you feel re-

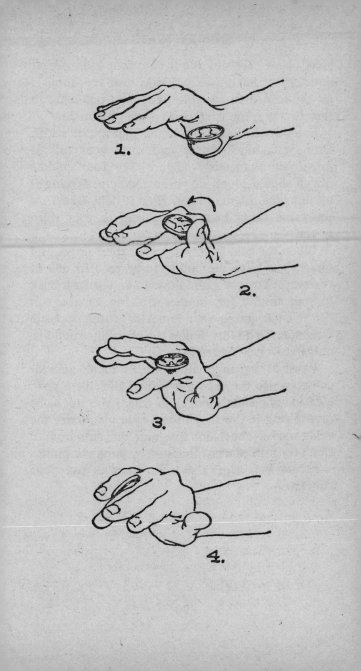

1.

2.

3.

4.

laxed. Now carefully flip it onto your index-finger knuckle so that the coin hangs over the knuckle on the middle-finger side. If it does not hang in this direction the trick won't work (figure 2).

Extend your fingers and keep your muscles stiff. Drop your index finger and raise your middle finger simultaneously (figure 3). Your middle finger should touch down on the coin, forcing it up onto the middle finger. Hold it now. Okay. Do the same thing to move the coin to your third finger.

When the coin is between your third finger and pinky, you have the option to proceed in one of two ways. You can palm the coin and bring it back to your thumb for another crossing, or you can flip it back across your knuckles in the opposite direction. To do this, follow the above instructions, only in reverse (figure 4).

Word of warning: since mostly tough guys or con-men use the coin roll in real life, it's a good idea to give some thought to where you might be seen trying it. Two additional safe places are the supermarket check-out line and the laundromat. Don't try it in places inhabited by punks or bullies —unless you can also roll them across your knuckles.

DO-IT-YOURSELF DECAPITATION

Stage magicians like to tell you that the hand is quicker than the eye. Like everything else about stage magicians, this proposition is illusory, as you know if you've ever practiced a sleight-of-hand trick and then had it fail because the audience just can't seem to keep from watching you very carefully.

The truth is, the professional magician succeeds where you fail because he has the power to direct your attention somewhere else while he is reaching up his sleeve for the rabbit. Now, cutting off your head with a piece of string depends upon a ridiculously simple manipulation of the string. Anybody who actually sees what you are doing will see right through the trick. But this is the case with almost every sleight-of-hand. What we're

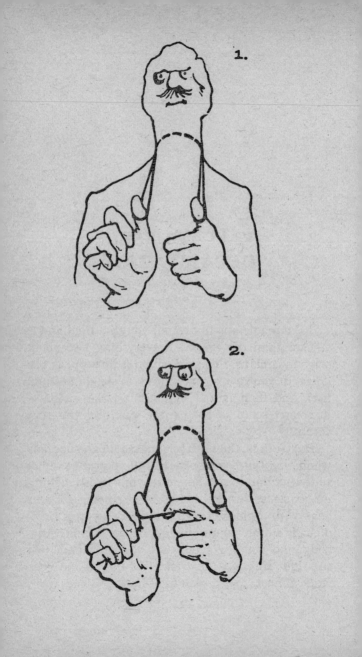

1.

2.

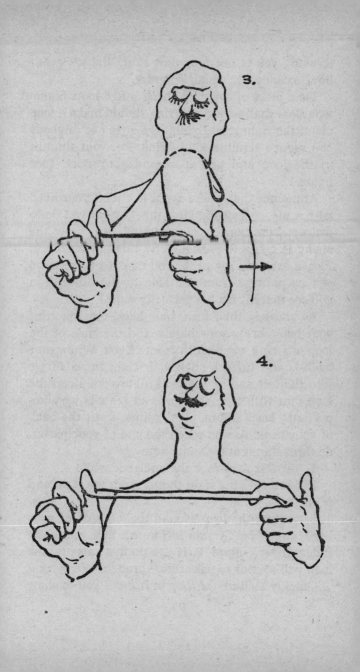

showing you is not only how to do the trick, but how to conceal it, which is harder.

Tie a piece of ordinary string into a loop. Somewhat less than a yard of string should make a loop about the right size. Exhibit the string so anybody can see it's genuine solid string. Put your thumbs in the loop and pull it around your neck (see figure 1).

Announce that you're about to cut off your head with a piece of string. Now this is what you do to distract attention: say something like "Now the string is going to pass directly through my neck. Please examine my neck. You can see there is no slot or passage from one side to the other. You will see that my neck is perfectly solid."

As you say this, turn your back. As you turn your back, bring your hands, and the ends of the loop of string, together in front of you. While your back is still turned, stick your right index finger into the left end of the loop (figure 2). Keep the loop taut with both thumbs, and (this is very important) keep talking all the time about the back of your neck. As you reach the end of your patter, do three things at the same time:

1. turn back to face the audience while

2. removing the right thumb from the right end of the loop, while

3. pulling the loop around the left side of your neck, supported by your left thumb and your right index finger (figure 3). If you do this smartly, the loop will appear to pass right through your neck.

Quickly hold up the loop in front of you to show

that it is unbroken (figure 4). Then hand it immediately to a spectator before somebody observes that the string is now looped, not between your thumbs, but between a thumb and an index finger. Shake your head to show that it doesn't fall off.

Remember two very important things; Never do the same trick twice, or somebody will see through it; and always find a way to get the audience to look somewhere else. Professional magicians distract the audience with showmanship, which requires talent; we've shown you how to do it by putting your back between the audience and the gimmick, which only requires nerve. Remember, the point of showing off is to look better, smarter and more highly skilled than in fact you are.

SPARE CHANGE?

Times being what they are, you probably don't have as much change in your pocket as you used to. That is, except if you have an oil well buried in your back yard. Not long ago, we met a fellow who has quite a few of them—and there was the clanking of coins in his robe to prove it. We chatted a while about the world situation, then the fellow produced some quarters and performed a feat that left us speechless. We are still speechless. So speechless, in fact, that we will let our chic sheik teach you the trick himself.

HERE'S A NEAT
LITTLE NUMBER
YOU CAN DO
WITH JUST SOME
SPARE CHANGE

BALANCE ONE OR
MORE COINS ON
YOUR ELBOW
LIKE THIS
THEN...

...IN ONE SWIFT
MOVE YOU BRING
YOUR FOREARM
FORWARD AND
CATCH THEM ALL.
NOW OFFER
THE COINS
TO A
FOLLOWER
TO DO
THE SAME.

HE, OF COURSE WILL
SPRAY THE COINS ALL
OVER THE TENT — NOT
KNOWING IT'S NECESSARY
TO BEND THE KNEES
AS YOU ARE MAKING
YOUR MOVE.

TWO TRICKS FOR A BUCK

Everyone talks about the shrinking dollar but nobody does anything about it. We will! Right now we'll show you how to get years of great entertainment out of a dollar bill—and it won't cost you a red cent!

We learned this feat from a show-off named Marjorie. It seems that for years she has been conspiring with her brother-in-law at family get-togethers. The brother-in-law, playing the straight man, says, "Let's see Marjorie cut a pencil in two with a dollar bill." Then Marjorie, a great entertainer if there ever was one, does just that. Here is how she does it.

Take a dollar bill, preferably a new, stiff one, and hold it in whichever hand is most comfortable. Fold the bill neatly in half, lengthwise, as shown

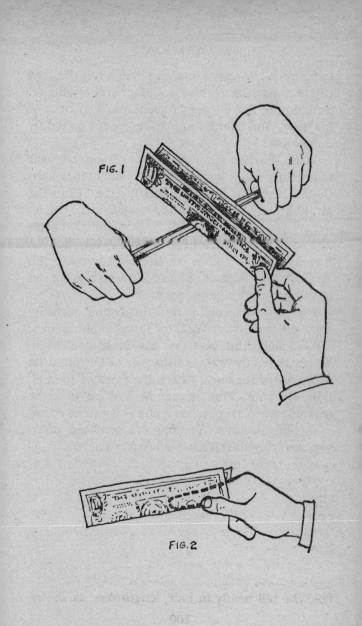

FIG. 1

FIG. 2

in figure 1. Now have someone hold a full-size lead pencil at each end with the thumb and forefinger. Tell him to hold the pencil about a foot in front of his body. And tell him to hold the pencil as tightly as possible.

With the hand holding the bill, extend your index finger so it looks like you're using it to keep the bill straight. But after you lift the bill in the air, and just before you strike it against the pencil, extend your index finger. It is the finger that actually cracks the pencil in two, not the bill. But the finger is hidden within the folds of the dollar bill and is never detected. Figure 2 shows the correct position of the finger within the bill.

Now for the second part of this twofer, a classic show-off maneuver. We'll try this one out on you. Take a dollar bill and find the mushroom in it. That's right, there's a mushroom to be found on every American buck. Check the front of the bill, now the back. Find it yet? No? Want to know where it is? We'll give you a clue—it can be found by folding George Washington's forehead down over his frilly shirt front. See? Yuk, yuk.

OFF WITH YOUR THUMB!

Going through life with our members intact is a goal we all share; but there are advantages to some detachable parts. Some day you may choose to sacrifice your toupee to save your life from wild Indians or, when exploring the Amazon basin, impress the natives with your strength and agility by popping your false teeth in and out. Even harsher measures have been tried; Vincent Van Gogh cut off one ear to please a lady, and went even crazier than he was when that didn't work.

A much safer arrangement, which has the virtue of being both painless and reversible, is to learn how to pull your thumb off and put it back at will. Before you go any further, we'd better make it perfectly clear—but only to you—that this is nothing but an illusion. Your thumb will only *appear*

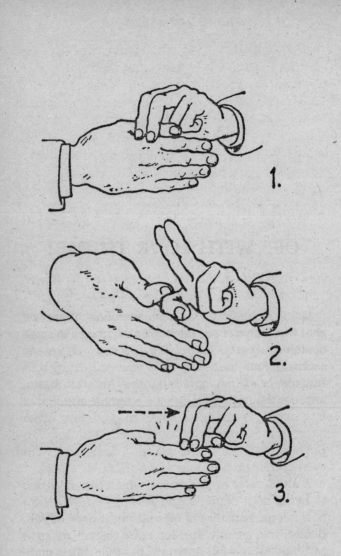

1.

2.

3.

to come off. But that's your secret and ours—to the world at large, you will appear to be the detach-able-thumb champion of the world.

A word of caution first: this trick has been known to make children cry and weak women faint, so watch it, because you don't want to be responsible for anybody's emotional condition but your own. But enough of the sincerity, just practice the following steps:

1. Present your left hand, covering the first joint of your left thumb with the first two fingers of your right hand, as in figure 1. It's a little hard to get attention in this position—you can't wave your hands around—so you may have to clear your throat and say something arresting like "Wanna see my old war wound?" or "I bet Robert Redford can't do this!" Hesitate a moment and check your positioning. Figure 2 shows the actual position of fingers and thumbs. Bend the left thumb as far out of the way as you can get it.

2. Pull your right hand to the left, taking with it what appears to be the end of your left thumb. Some pull it off with a mighty roar and an appearance of great effort, but in our opinion this detracts from the effect; the best way is to just nonchalantly slide the thing off. Then, before anybody has a chance to figure out what you're up to, slide it back on.

Pick up any fainting women from the floor, and try to soothe the weeping children, but be sure not to do the same stunt before the same audience another time, no matter how much they ask you. People will catch on, and the great object of a life like ours is to always keep them guessing.

CRUSHING A BEER CAN
WITH YOUR BARE HAND

We are talking here about a steel beer can, not that new aluminum kind. Aluminum is for sissies, and everybody knows it.

Contrary to popular belief, crushing a beer can with one hand does not require strength. Brute strength will do it, sure, but the point of showing off is to do more and better things than your natural endowments allow (which is probably not much to begin with). Properly done, the trick lies in the technique.

Why crush beer cans? you might wonder. First, it flattens them and keeps them from rolling noisily down church or railroad-car aisles. More important, crushing beer cans is a terrific way to get attention on the beach or at a fraternity party. Extra points are won by laying waste to a vast

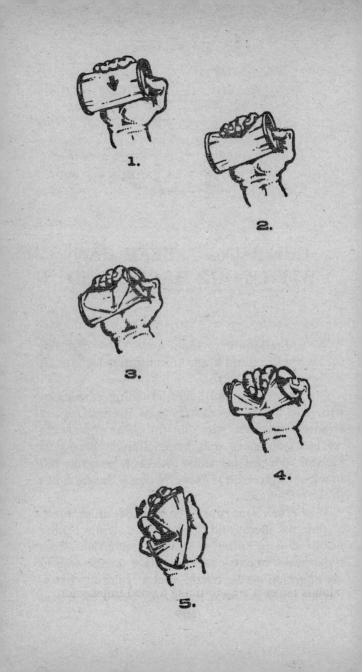

1.

2.

3.

4.

5.

number of cans throughout an afternoon or evening. Remember that you yourself must drink the beer from all cans you endeavor to crush. Don't go around picking up other people's cans. It simply doesn't look good. Ready now?

1. Hold the can in whichever hand is most comfortable. The ends of the can should be equidistant from the point at which the can rests on your palm (figure 1).

2. Place your middle finger on the can's midpoint and squeeze firmly with the middle finger, backed up with the third and index fingers (figure 2). Make a slight dent, but be careful not to dent the opposite, palm side of the can.

3. Deepen the crease until it is about one-third of the can's diameter. The crease should be perpendicular to the length of the can and equidistant from each end. As you deepen the crease, begin to rotate the can slightly (figure 3).

4. Exert more force with your fingers. Keep it up until the valley of the crease is a quarter-inch from the palm side of the can (which should still be smooth and unbuckled). Now, shifting your grip if necessary, squeeze the ends of the can toward each other until the can begins to fold up (figure 4).

5. Push the ends of the can together until they touch (figure 5).

Practice the procedure until it all takes but a few seconds. If there is a trash barrel nearby, throw the crushed can into it. Don't litter—being a slob is never a way to make a good impression.

WHISTLING
WITH TWO FINGERS

Whistling with two fingers is a sure way to get the attention of taxis, horses and dogs. It produces a shriller, more impressive noise than whistling without fingers. It also looks nicer, and gives the whistler more authority, because if you whistle without fingers people may not notice that you are the source of the earsplitting racket. Here's how:

1. Place the tips of your forefingers together (figure 1). Some people use four fingers, though the principle is the same. The four-finger technique employs the middle and index finger of each hand.

2. Keeping the fingertips together, place them just under the tip of your tongue and raise it slightly. Push the tongue backward until your lips close on the first knuckles of your fingers (figure

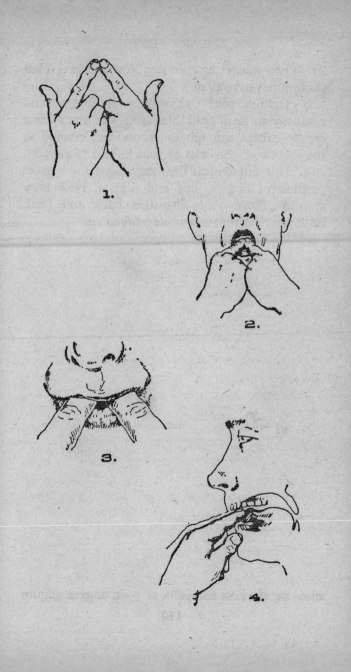

2). When mastering this step, use a mirror (but make sure you're alone).

3. Tighten your lips over your fingers and against your teeth until there is no way that air can escape except through the sound-box created in the V between the ends of your fingers (figure 3).

4. This anatomical drawing shows the correct position of fingers, lips and tongue. Now blow steadily. Move your fingertips back and forth until you hear that first wonderful chirp.

HOW TO BE VERY, VERY INCOMBUSTIBLE

A show-off rarely or never goes to cocktail parties. There are many excellent reasons for this reluctance, some social (cocktail parties are boring), some moral (cocktail parties are wicked), some medical (tobacco, alcohol and talking too loud are bad for your health sooner or later). But the most important reason for staying away is egotistical: eventually everybody at a cocktail party starts showing off, and that means it's going to be hard for you to get the attention you deserve. Your message will become lost and fuzzed in the social static.

Nevertheless, suppose that, much against your will, you find yourself at a cocktail party with one of those cold things in your hand and somebody blowing cigarette smoke into your earholes. What

you have to do is make the best of it, and the best
you can make of it is to show yourself not only
sober but fireproof. Politely but aggressively you
approach the man or woman with the cigarette
and ask: "What is that thing you're smoking?"

"Why, it's a Brand X," he/she replies.

"May I see it?" you inquire in a winning voice.

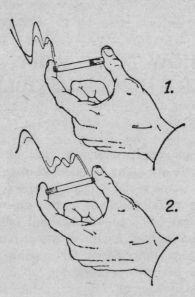

"Of course," is the response you anticipate.
What you do next is, you pick the cigarette up between your thumb and forefinger, as shown in
figure 1, and you just hold it for a while. Then
you turn it around and hold it the other way
round (figure 2). Then after you've made your
point, you hand it back.

Now, how did you do this without getting burned? Easy. Remember the cold thing in your hand? It was a glass full of ice and something, no doubt. You held it for a long time—maybe fifteen minutes, until your fingertips were very cold. Every time your fingers warmed the spot on the glass beneath them, you rotated the glass to a fresh cold place. What's more, the condensation on the glass coated your fingers with a film of water. Only when your fingertips were thoroughly chilled did you venture to pick up the hot coal of the cigarette —and because the heat flow from the cigarette took a while to warm your fingers up to an uncomfortable temperature, you didn't get burned. In fact, if your fingers were damp enough, the cigarette just plain went out before you handed it back. That showed them, didn't it?

A word of warning: fire will burn if you overdo it. When you begin to feel the heat, get rid of the cigarette. Two or three seconds is plenty to prove that you're made of the very best asbestos.

Part Three:

Arts and Crafty

HOW TO MAKE
CUSTOM-MADE MONEY

In these hard times it is getting more and more difficult to have a lot of money. But it's easy to look like you do. In fact, you can even give the impression that you have your cash custom-made.

Go to the bank and get fifty new dollar bills, as crisp as the bank can give you. Go home and make ready an empty checkbook cover, preferably one with your name stamped on the front. Also, make ready the empty cardboard that once held the checks in place. Such a cardboard is shown in figure 1, page 120.

Cut a strip of gauze to fit the edge of cardboard. Now, with glue—we recommend rubber cement—coat the gauze and adhere it to the edge of the cardboard, as in figure 2.

Keeping your stack of bills in a neat pile, carefully stick them to the edge of the cardboard. Set aside to dry. Then, insert the cardboard into your personalized cover and close it.

All this comes in handy the next time you go up to a cashier to pay a bill or check. Tear out the necessary number of bills without giving the impression this is in any way strange. You, God bless you, come out looking like one rich dude!

THE SHOW-OFF
PAPER AIRPLANE

Everybody knows how to make some kind of paper airplane. The difference between everybody and a show-off is that the show-off knows what a paper airplane is good for. The purpose of a paper airplane is not to fly well. As an aerodynamic vehicle, no paper airplane is very good and most are lousy. Those who, in spite of our advice, want to build paper airplanes that fly less badly than others may read and profit by *Scientific American's Great Paper Airplane Book,* available from your bookseller; but that's not, we repeat, the purpose of paper airplanes.

The purpose of paper airplanes is to attract attention and register boredom. Wherever a lot of people are gathered together working with paper, most of them aren't really working at all. What better way to annoy the few who are actually busy than by making and flying a truly elaborate paper airplane? In fact, it's better if you don't fly it, because that shows you're only making it because you have nothing better to do. For this purpose, the more elaborate the paper airplane the better, and here's the most elaborate we know. Just follow these few simple instructions, and you'll get a paper airplane that flies well enough if you really insist.

Take a piece of 8½ by 11 inch typing paper and fold it diagonally to make a square (figure 1). Crease the portion that remains at the bottom and tear off, but do not discard. Crease the square along the opposite diagonal as well, then crease it straight across the middle (figure 2).

Fold the left and right sides together till they meet. The end result of this step is a triangle with the point at the bottom, as shown in figure 3.

The triangle is really two layers thick. Take the top layer at one end and fold down to the point at the bottom, as shown on the left side of figure 4. Then repeat for the right side.

Fold one more time to the center, as shown on the left side of figure 5; repeat for the right side.

Now return to the extra strip you tore off in the beginning. Crease a V down its middle, then tear it into the shape shown in figure 6 to serve as the tail of the airplane. The pointed end at left should match the point at the bottom of the triangle as shown in figure 5.

Take the tail and stick it inside the triangle (we

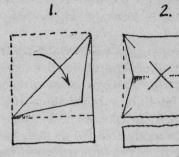

1.

2.

3.

4.

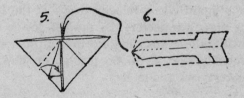

5.

6.

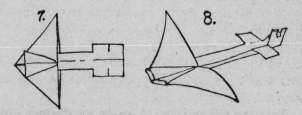

7.

8.

might as well call it the wing now) at the point shown in figure 5. Now the whole thing should look like figure 7.

Carefully keeping the tail in place, rip from the point of the nose backwards down the middle of the plane. Stop ripping when you have reached the front of the fat little subordinate triangles you made in step 5. Then take the nose, which is now torn into two sections, fold the sections back, and stuff them into those two little triangles. This gives you the blunt nose shown in the final illustration. Fold the tail as shown.

Now you have it. It adds stability to crease the wing just a little bit, giving it a slight dihedral angle. The plane may be glided softly out a high window, or for altitude you can hold it by the nose, placing your forefinger down the middle of the wing, and heave it; the tail collapses, but snaps back again when velocity drops at the height of the plane's trajectory. By now, if you've been following these instructions in your office, you've probably been fired. So just go on down to the nearest park and let fly.

GROWING A CARROT
UPSIDE DOWN

We all live now in the Golden Age of House-plants. Ecological consciousness surrounds us from right and from left, and every windowsill in the nation is full of green growing stuff, from moss to mushrooms.

The show-off should, of course, have bigger and better house plants than other people, but how to grow house plants is itself a book-length subject we won't go into here (though we could, of course) so we trust you to look out for yourself mostly. We'll just have to be content with showing you how to grow a carrot upside down into a green and leafy little urn, suspended neatly in the window by a piece of string. We'll bet everybody else on your block grows his carrots right-side-up.

Get the biggest carrot you can find, and wash it

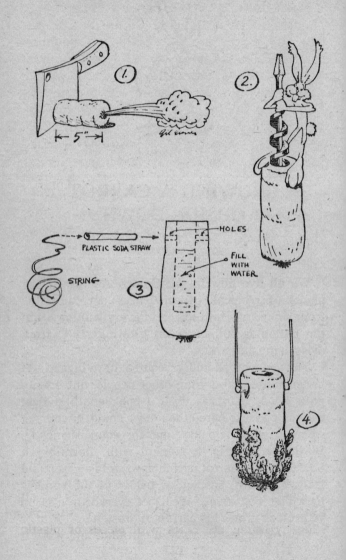

1.

← 5" →

2.

PLASTIC SODA STRAW →

STRING

3.

HOLES

FILL WITH WATER

4.

nice and clean. Then lay it on the chopping block and neatly cut it off a convenient length from the green end (figure 1). Four or five inches should be enough except in the case of the largest carrots. Peel the other end and eat it.

Now, make a hole in your piece of carrot. Use any convenient kind of hole-maker; a woodworking bit of the right size, held in the hand, is about the neatest way (figure 2). Hole out your carrot until you have a cross-section like figure 3.

Punch a couple of holes an inch or so from the top (we are going to call the green end the bottom from now on) of the carrot, and thread a piece of string through. Hang it up in a sunny window. Fill up the carrot with water.

In a few days green things will begin to sprout (figure 4). In a few more days they will start to grow upward. In a couple of months, if you remember to keep turning the carrot around, they will grow into a sort of ferny green urn-shaped gob of foliage around the carrot.

The only things to watch out for are these: first, as your carrot grows more and more leaves it will require more and more water daily. Don't ever let it dry out. Second, the flesh of the carrot above water level is bound to wither some, and as it does the strings will begin cutting upwards from the holes you put them in. Eventually the carrot will be sliced through and you'll have to start with a fresh carrot, but you can delay this moment somewhat by lining the holes with pieces of plastic soda straw, or some kind of appropriate grommets, or something; you figure out what kind.

Finally, it probably won't hurt if once a month or so you mix up some soluble fertilizer. Follow the instructions on the package—only use about half as much as it says—and water the carrot with this instead of plain water.

THE NEWSPAPER TREE

If you read books, chances are you read newspapers, which is in itself a most enjoyable and educational experience. But what do you do when you're finished? Well, if everyone else in the family has read the paper, why not learn one of the great old tricks that needs as raw material only the paper itself? In case you don't know how, here is how to make a glorious tree out of a newspaper, which is better for the ecology than the other way around.

Using the full length of the paper, tear off two strips not less than ten or twelve inches wide. Then, with one inside the other and overlapping the other by a couple of inches, gently roll them up.

Take the rolled strips and, with a scissors or

neatly with your fingers, make a series of incisions lengthwise, about five of them. Your roll should look like figure 2.

Make sure that your incisions come about midway down the roll. Your tree is now ready to sprout. This step, particularly if you're trying to impress children, should be executed with a grand flourish. Holding the uncut roll in one hand, use your other hand to take the center of the roll and pull up on it. Pull gently so you don't rip the roll or disturb the incisions. Your tree should look more or less like the tree in figure 3.

You can now use the rest of the paper to create an entire forest of trees, or simply plant the first in the corner of your room and watch to see if it grows. If it doesn't, try talking to it—some say that helps.

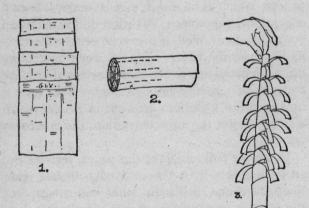

SECRETS OF
THE WATER BOMB

When America was young and ingenious, college kids—and kids even younger than that—used to create, from mere pieces of paper, containers to fill with water and drop on each other from dormitory windows and other high places. Paper was used because milk bottles were heavy enough to be dangerous and rubber balloons were too expensive. Today, the wheel has come full circle—milk doesn't arrive in bottles, but in plastic or paper containers folded by vast impersonal machines. Return now to those thrilling days of yesteryear, and learn how to make a paper water-bomb; and when your destructive impulses are satisfied, you will find that with just a tug here and a pull there, the water-bomb snaps into a perfect cube, useful for building castles along the edge of your desk.

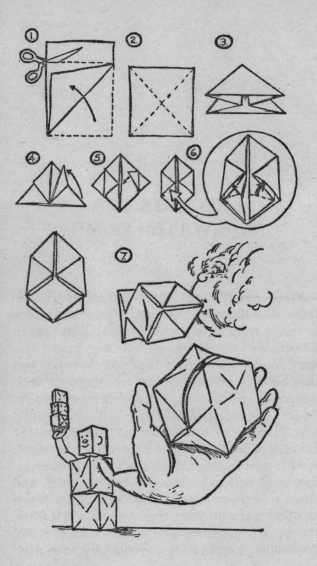

Start by folding a sheet of paper on its diagonal and cutting off the excess material to get a perfect square (figure 1). Crease the square thus obtained in both directions between corners (figure 2) and then collapse two opposite sides (not corners) inwards, toward each other, to obtain the triangular shape shown in figure 3.

Now lift one of the bottom points of the triangle and fold it upward toward the top of the triangle, as shown on the right-hand side of figure 4. Do the same with the opposite point; when finished, it will resemble the left-hand side of figure 4.

Turn the paper over and do the same with the lower points of the triangle on the other side. You now have a square on end, the same shape and orientation as a baseball diamond. Take the points at left and right—first and third base—and fold to the center (figure 5). Turn over and do the same on the other side, to attain the shape shown in the small drawing in figure 6.

Now comes the tricky part. There are a pair of little loose triangular flaps at the bottom of the developing water-bomb. Lift them, crease them across the middle, away from you, and insert into the spaces shown in the flaps above them, as the detail drawing in figure 6 illustrates. Turn over and do the same on the other side.

You now have figure 7. The water-bomb is finished, and needs only to be inflated to be ready for use. Of course, you may store the collapsed units in any convenient space until ready. It remains only to blow briskly through the open end of the bomb to inflate it. Then fill it up with water and wait for a passerby, or just tug at the corners with your fingers until it snaps into a perfect cube. Pile them up as high as you like, then invite the neighbors in.

STEPPING THROUGH
A SMALL PIECE OF PAPER

Let's say you're sitting in your office, classroom, or living room, totally fed up with what's going on around you, which is probably nothing at all. You pick up a small piece of paper, no more than six inches square, and say to the person next to you, "Hey, I bet you $100,000 I can step right through this small piece of paper, even pull it over my entire body, all the way over my head." Very cute, they say, then dare you. So you do. They stare. They gape. They burst into extended applause. Maybe, even, they lose a small bet. Here's how:

The piece of paper should be as small as possible—but no less than six inches per side. Nonchalantly fold the paper in half (figures 1 and 2, page 136).

With a scissors, or tearing with your fingers,

make a slit every half-inch or so. Alternate the slits so that one starts on the folded side, the next on the open side (figure 3).

After you've made your slits, cut or tear along the folded side, making sure you do not cut or tear the fold at the top or bottom of the paper (see figure 3).

When you're all finished, look your victim right in the eye, then unfold your little piece of paper. It will open up into an enormous, glorious ring (figure 4).

Now put the ring down on the floor, step inside, and pull it up over your body, then over your noggin. Collect your winnings with a smile and, when the chump asks what you do for an encore, play dumb (and deaf).

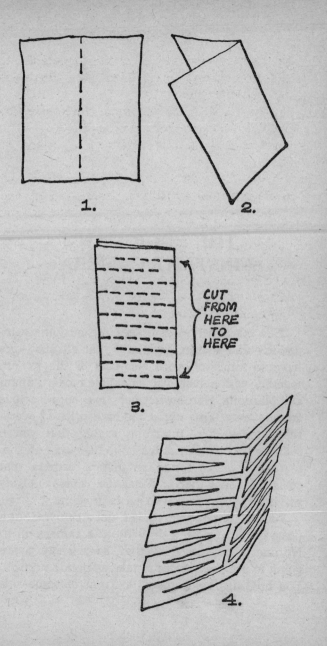

1.

2.

CUT
FROM
HERE
TO
HERE

3.

4.

THE POOR MAN'S
INSTANT CAMERA

This construction combines the customary ingenuity and manual dexterity that all show-offs have so much of, with elements of the put-on, together with a dash of fashionable modern financial planning. Here's what happens: suppose your friends are talking about the high price of everything today. You interrupt, saying that you've found a way to beat at least the high cost of photography; you've found an instant camera that costs a lot less than a dollar. Of course, nobody will believe this, so you've got to prove it.

You pull out of your pocket, not a camera, but a piece of paper with a drawing of a camera on it. No one is impressed by that, so you say you're going to use the camera to take a friend's portrait. You hold up the "camera" in front of someone's face and ask him to watch the birdie. You give a quick snap to the paper and ZIP! where the "camera" was is now a cartoon face—his "portrait." If this makes your friend so angry he tears up the camera and stomps on it, that's all right, because you can make another one in a few minutes. Here's how:

1. Take a piece of paper about twice as long as it is wide—say 6 by 12 inches—and fold it across the middle, into two identical more-or-less-square halves.

2. Decide where the corners of the "camera" are going to be, and punch four holes with a sharp pencil through both halves of the folded paper. If you don't like the marks the pencil leaves, use a pin; just be sure that the holes are identically located on both halves of the folded paper.

3. Unfold the paper and lay it flat, with the side that was inside the fold down. With a sharp knife or scissors, cut vertical slits between the top and bottom holes on each half of the paper, as shown in figure 3; then cut a horizontal slit between the lower pair of holes on each half of the paper. You now have a loose flap on each half of the paper, with the loose edge at the bottom. On the lower half of the paper, draw a funny face, keeping it all inside the edges of the flap. Outside the flap, draw the body of the camera and add a tripod, a squeeze-bulb and, if you like, a birdie for authenticity. When you're finished with this step, the paper should resemble figure 3.

1. FOLD
2.
3.
4.
5.

4. Turn the paper over, being sure to turn it left-to-right, not end-for-end. Inside the top flap, draw the lens and bellows of the camera as shown in figure 4.

5. Fold the paper back the way it was in step 2. The funny face is now exposed on the front of the "camera." To load the camera, open up the paper a little and tuck the "lens" forward, while you tuck the funny face backwards. The bellows and lens overlap the funny face through the hole in the paper, and now appear on the front of the camera as in figure 5. The camera is now loaded and ready to take a comic picture of anyone.

Now, to shoot the camera, just open and shut the folded paper about halfway in a quick, snappy motion. The lens disappears and funny face jumps into view. Go find your best friend and photograph him before the film goes stale. It's true this instant camera has limitations—everybody tends to look alike and, even worse, everybody looks even uglier than usual.

WORLD'S GREATEST
CAT'S CRADLE

Once upon a time, everybody knew how to make elaborate cat's cradles. Like a lot of other manual skills, this too is passing, which is bad for America but good for the show-off. The less everybody else knows, the more brightly does the knowledge of the show-off shine.

Not only are cat's cradles very pretty, they require only a piece of string and two idle hands, articles very easy to come by these days. The next time you see a piece of string being used for some sensible purpose, like package wrapping, interrupt the whole activity by seizing the string, and become the center of attention by producing this magnificent cat's cradle.

Look at figure 9, page 144, to see what you're going to get. Splendid, yes? All right, here's how to get it. Follow these instructions carefully, and be sure at all times that you're handling only the strings we tell you to; otherwise, horrible confusion will crop up. Ready?

Take a piece of string not less than six feet long, preferably seven, and tie it into a loop. Pick up the loop with both hands, as shown in figure 1 (all illustrations are drawn from your own point of view), with the string crossing the palms between finger and thumb.

With your right index finger, reach over to your left palm and pick up the string on the back of the finger (figure 2). Pull the string taut by separating your hands. Now do the exact reverse action with your left hand, resulting in figure 3. You now have a loop of string over each index finger.

Without disturbing the other strings, reach over with your right hand, pick the loop off your left index finger, and drop it over your left wrist. Pull taut, do the exact reverse action with the left hand working on the right, and pull taut again. Now things have reached the state shown in figure 4.

You now have a loop over each pinky, each thumb, and each wrist. With the right hand, grab the string just in front of the left pinky, pull out a little slack, draw the string across the left palm, and drop it over the left thumb, creating a new loop over the thumb. Then, with the right hand, grab the string that was already there on the left thumb—not the one you just put there—grasping it on the opposite side of the thumb from your face, pull out some slack, and drop it over the left

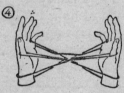
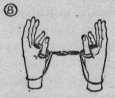
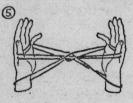
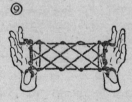

pinky (refer to the left hand of figure 5 to see how the strings ought to go). Now repeat exactly, using the left hand to work on the right-hand strings. You should now have figure 5.

Now, see where all those strings come together in the middle of figure 5? Seize the whole bunch right in the middle with your left hand and lay them over the crotch of your right thumb onto the back of your right hand (figure 6). You will see that there are two loops of string around your right thumb; carefully grab both loops with your left hand, pull them straight up off the right thumb, and keep hold of them while allowing the whole mess of string on the back of your right hand to pass upward and clear of your right thumb (figure 7). Then, with your left hand, put the two loops you're holding back on your right thumb, just the way they were. Now do the same thing exactly, using your right hand, to the strings on your left hand. You have now attained figure 8.

Using your right hand, reach over your left hand, pick up the loop around your left wrist, pull it up and over your left hand, let go, dropping the string into the middle between your hands. Do the same thing with your left hand to the loop of string around your right wrist.

Now the amazing part happens. Draw the string taut by separating your hands and there you are: figure 9! That's if you've been very careful to follow the instructions and not dropped any strings. If you don't have figure 9, go back and start over, because it's in the string waiting for you to find it.

THE ART OF
SELF-UGLIFICATION

It seems probable that primitive man's first show-off trick was to make a nasty face. Primitive man just stuck out his tongue and crossed his eyes; civilization taught him to draw out the corners of his mouth with his pinky fingers while shoving his nose upward with his thumbs. Nowadays, technology and imagination allow the use of artificial aids in face-making. With the three simple devices we're about to show you, you'll be able to make a face so nasty your mother will rue the day you were taught to read. Here goes, in three easy steps.

1. Walnut Monster Eyes:

Obtain a large English walnut and carefully divide it into two perfect halves. Eat the meat, and clean out the inside of each half of the shell with sandpaper until there are no rough edges. Then take a twist drill of one-eighth inch diameter or smaller and bore a hole dead in the middle of each shell (figure 1). Put the shells in your eyes, monocle fashion, crinkling the cheeks slightly if necessary to hold them in place. You should be able to see out pretty well. Now look in a mirror. Revolting!

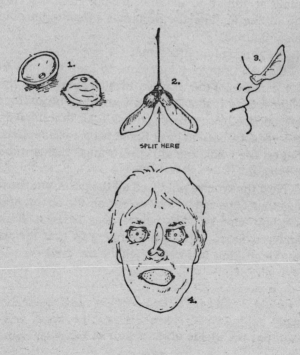

SPLIT HERE

2. Green Nose Thing:

Get a fresh green maple seed (of course you have to wait until they are falling from the trees in your neighborhood). Maple seeds are the kind that look like figure 2.

Break off one half of the maple seed and throw it away. Take the other and, using a sharp finger-nail or a paring knife, split the seed end, leaving the flying-wing end intact. As long as the seed was fresh and green to start with, the inside of the seed will be all sticky—sticky enough that you can make it adhere to the end of your nose, sticking up in the air like the proboscis of some horrible bug (figure 3).

3. Orange Monolith Teeth:

Peel an orange, taking care to keep the peel in large pieces. Find a piece of the peel that's the right size to insert between your lips but in front of your teeth, so when you smile all that appears is a hideous orange grin. Some people use lemons, but on the whole the effect of orange peel is more interesting.

Now that you've practiced all the parts, put them together (figure 4). Now go out on the street, and see how long it takes before dogs begin to bark and you hear that distant siren wail that means you're striking terror throughout the city!

Part Four:

So You Want to Be a Stuntman

A DRUGSTORE COWBOY
LASSOS AN ICE CUBE

This little number combines the show-off properties of ice cubes with the show-off properties
of string—both articles easy to find, but not usually found in the same place at the same time,
except in old-fashioned general stores with soda
fountains. In order to score prestige points by
lassoing an ice cube, it's usually necessary to
carry the string with you down to the drugstore
counter and order the glass of water separately.
The string should be the cotton kind, fibrous and
easy to soak with water—positively not the new-
fangled nylon or synthetic sort that hardly gets
wet at all.

So, here's what you do. You tie a one-or-two-
inch loop in the end of the piece of string, sit down
at the counter, and ask for a glass of ice water.

The ice has to be in cubes, of course. Then you ask your nearest neighbor if he thinks he can remove the ice cube from the water by using the loop of string. He is not allowed to touch the glass with his fingers, or indeed to move the glass in any way. If you've picked a sensible victim, his most probable response will be: "No, I can't, and you can't either." Your only way out of this dilemma is to insist in a firm voice that you can so. Try to sound positive. Make him believe it. Then let him try (figure 1).

After he's tried and failed long enough, then you step in. Your secret, of course, is that you cheat. You simply lower the loop onto the exposed top surface of the floating ice cube, so it just lies there on top of the cube. Try to get it to lie as flat as you can. Then, take a pinch of salt and sprinkle it on top of the ice cube, string and all (figure 2). Wait a few seconds. The action of the salt on the ice cube will freeze the string solid to the cube. Then all you have to do is pick it up (figure 3). Astounding! Of course, you probably won't want to drink the water after this. If your victim objects that you didn't say you were going to use salt in this trick, the best answer is that you didn't say you weren't.

This can also be done with a toothpick—the flat kind, not the round torpedo-shaped product—by simply adding water to the glass until the top of the ice cube is level with the top of the glass. The toothpick is then rested on the rim of the glass and the ice cube, and the end of it that's on the cube is salted. Seconds later, you can pick up the cube using the toothpick as a handle. It works just as well this way, but the string method is more spectacular, and the show-off, given any kind of choice, always prefers the flashy by a wide margin.

HOW TO BE A
TWENTY-CARD WIZARD

Everybody knows some kind of card trick; the difference between a show-off's superior card trick and an ordinary citizen's hum-drum everyday card trick lies, in this case, in sheer magnitude. Allowing one person to pick a card, and then correctly identifying it, is impressive; two is better; three is astonishing; but today's mastermind manipulation permits the show-off to allow up to ten people to pick cards, and then spot them all correctly. It boggles—think of the glory!—ten minds at once. Of course, if you can't find ten willing participants, it works just as well with fewer, down to and including one.

The effect is this: You shuffle a deck of cards (or let anyone else shuffle it) as much as you like and then deal ten pairs face down—a total of twenty

cards in stacks of two. You turn your back or leave the room or offer to be blindfolded while your victims choose pairs, pick them up, examine them, memorize them, and put them back down—in any order at all, provided the pairs stay together. You re-enter the room, pick up all the pairs, and lay them out face up in four rows of five cards each. You ask any participant in the stunt to tell you which of the four rows his cards are in. If he tells the truth, you are able instantly to pick up the two cards he selected, and hand them to him. He retires in awe and embarrassment, and you proceed to do the same with as many participants as are on hand. Of course, if you're showing off to the full ten players, there will be only two cards left when you get to number ten, so he may not be as astonished as number one. O.K., here's how you do it:

To be a twenty-card wizard, you must memorize the following chart of four magic words:

ATLAS
BIBLE
THIGH
GOOSE

Notice that there are ten letters used in these four words, that each letter is used only twice, and that each word contains one and only one pair of letters: two A's in ATLAS, and so on. This should give you a clue as to how the trick actually works. The best way to learn the chart is to practice by getting a big sheet of paper and drawing the chart full-size—large enough to lay one card on top of each letter.

Now, clear the table and begin to practice. Deal ten pairs of cards face down. Impersonate a spectator by looking at one pair and memorizing it. Now pick up all the pairs into a stack, turn it face up, and lay out the cards face up on the chart like this: put the first card you come to on one of the A's in ATLAS; the second card, on the other A. The next card goes on one of the T's; the next, on the other T. The next two cards are placed on the

L's; the next two, on the S's; and so on. This will be a slow, awkward process at first. Do not lose heart. Your object is to learn to do it quickly, gracefully, and finally, without using an actual chart but working from your memory.

Now, when you have all the cards laid out, look for the two you picked. Whatever they were, they'll be on top of a pair of letters. If, say, they are in the first and fourth rows, they have to be the cards on S. If they are both in the second row, they have to be the cards on B; and so on.

When you have the chart thoroughly memorized, go forth and seek a roomful of suckers. Deal the pairs, and let your victims select one card pair each; lay out the cards according to the magic words ATLAS, BIBLE, THIGH, GOOSE. Do not, of course, be so careless as to whisper the words aloud, but store them safely in your memory. Ask the players to show you which row their cards are in. Unerringly you pick the right ones, thereby making up to ten people wish they, too, could be show-offs in the same class as yourself.

THE CALCULATED
SHOW-OFF

All a person really needs to show off is a wonderfully warped sense of him/herself. Very rarely is extra equipment necessary. This time, though, we'll tell you how to get some mileage out of those new-fangled pocket calculators that you see advertised on TV.

Take a pocket calculator and hand it to a friend or a sucker. Tell him to enter the number 8777 and multiply it by four. Ask him what he's got. When he tells you, tell him he's wrong. Tell him he's got the capital of Idaho. When he tells you you're nuts, take the calculator and turn it upside down. There, spelled out in what may easily pass for letters of the alphabet, is B O I S E. Get it?

Most numbers on the calculator, when looked at upside down, resemble letters of the alphabet, like this:

1 2 3 4 5 7 8 9 0
I Z E h S L B G O

You may not believe this if you don't have a calculator in front of you; when you do, however, you'll see what we mean.

What other unbelievable stunts can you do with the calculator? Tell another chump that your calculator can actually bring an oil company to his house. Tell him to enter the number 710.77345. When he looks at you funny, turn the machine over and show him what's what (as in the drawing here). He may think you're crazy but at least he'll respect you. Other calculating ideas to try: 0.7734 equals HELLO; 4509 equals GOSH; 2572 plus 87 times 12 equals the nickname of the male lead in "Casablanca."

Finally, one more trick. Ask your chump to enter his age on the calculator, then double it. Now, add 5 and multiply by 50. Tell him to add the amount of change in his pocket, up to a dollar. Now, subtract the number of days in a year, add 115, divide by 100. Your result will be his age, then a decimal, then the amount of change in his pocket. We've checked it and it works. If you try and it doesn't, don't blame us.

A RIDICULOUS
TEST OF STRENGTH

All show-offs are outer-directed people. It's impossible to show off without an audience. Nothing, therefore, gives us greater pleasure than to tell you about a fellow show-off, Dominic Valentine. Dominic lives in Philadelphia, where he employs the following stunt to win bets in bars. We don't recommend it to everybody, since, as you shall see, there is an element of risk involved, not to mention an element of looking awfully dumb if you fail. Later on we'll give you a foolproof method of showing your strength. But first, here's how Dominic proves that he's the strongest man in any bar in Philadelphia:

1. He obtains a willing subject (hopefully one who's not awfully big), gets him to lie down on the floor, and has him tighten his belt as snug as pos-

sible, with the excess belt sticking straight out in front.

2. He then leans over the subject's middle, placing both hands, palms down, just above the knees, as in football set position. He instructs the subject to fold his arms across his chest and to hold his body rigid, no matter what. Having checked to see that the belt is strong, and without a lot of stretch

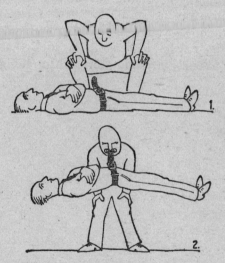

in it, he takes a comfortable amount of the subject's belt between his teeth.

3. He then clamps down on the belt and begins to rise.

We haven't met Dominic Valentine personally—he wrote us a letter about all this—but, to tell the truth, we're scared of him.

If you haven't got what it takes to pull people off the floor with your teeth—or don't especially want to find out if you do—here's a deceitful test of strength you'll always win:

1. Place your fingertips together in front of your chest.

2. Challenge the strongest man around to seize your arms just above the elbows and pull your fingers apart. No jerking, just steady pressure, applied any way he wants to (use of feet not allowed). Unless you're too puny to be reading this book, the mechanical set-up is such that you'll be able to resist anybody short of King Kong.

THE ENCHANTED BOAT

Three-fourths of the surface of the earth is water, so there's no telling where the show-off may run into a glass of the stuff. If you drink it, well and good. But when you've had enough, you're sure to begin playing with it, using it to impress your friends and vex your enemies. This little jape is almost self-explanatory, once we've explained it, but the solution is not likely to occur out of a blue sky. You might even use it to win a bet or two; we'll leave the set-up and the patter to you, but here's the elementary physics of the thing:

Start with a glass of water, almost full to the top (but not quite), and hand it, with a sort of cock-eyed smile, to the audience of your choice (figure 1, page 166).

Fashion a tiny boat of any available material.

165

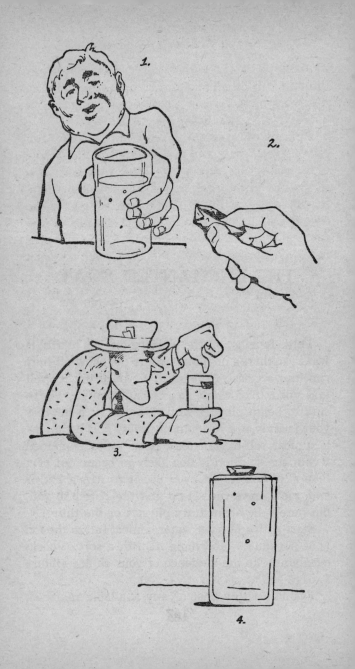

Actually it doesn't have to be a boat, just something that will float high on the water, but in practice what works best is a boat-shaped object bent out of a little bit of tin foil, like figure 2.

Drop the boat on the surface of the water and challenge all comers to make it stay in the middle of the glass. Don't worry. No matter how hard anyone tries, or how often they push it to the middle, it will always float off-center and adhere to the side of the glass (figure 3). Why? Because of the surface tension of the water is why; the phenomenon known as capillarity, which you can look up in the encyclopedia, forces it to the side every time. Now, place your bet that you and you alone can make the boat stay in the middle.

All right, the pay-off. Fill up the glass above the rim (figure 4). If your muscles are steady enough to do this free-hand, well and good; if you have trouble, do it by filling the glass as high as you can and then gently dropping pennies or something in. You'll be surprised how high you can stack the water in a bulge on top of the glass. The boat, to everyone's great satisfaction, now moves to the center of the glass and stays there.

Now that you've won, prove what a good sport you are by ordering a round of water for the whole table!

HOW TO PUSH A PENCIL
WITH YOUR MIND

A strong mind can do just about anything, though it can't move a mountain. It can, however, move a pencil across a table, and that's a fact. With the help of our brilliant assistant shown here, we will teach you how to move a pencil across a surface, without ever touching it.

In figure 1, our assistant holds up an ordinary pencil. For purposes that will remain a secret, make sure you use a round pencil, not one with edges.

In figure 2, our assistant begins summoning his strong mind to action. This is achieved by shaking the hands and arms. This action activates the very complicated "force-fields" that will ultimately move the pencil.

In figure 3 our assistant begins to circle the pen-

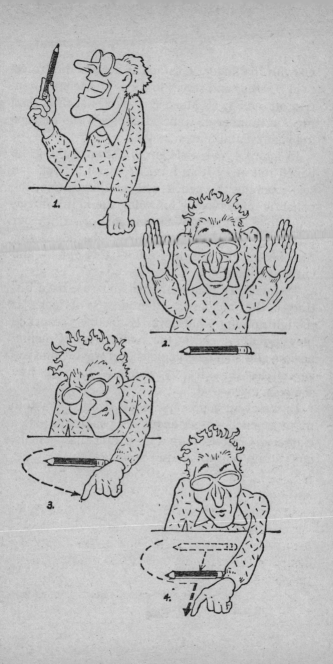

1.

2.

3.

4.

cil with his finger. This action defines the "force-field" further and serves to focus all mental attention on the object. Make slow circles at first; then make a number of frenzied circles while increasing your mental concentration.

In figure 4, our assistant is shown making the pencil roll away from him. He is not, as you can see, touching the pencil with his hands. No, the pencil is miraculously following the man's finger, no strings attached. Well, one sort of string: our assistant is gently blowing air on the table's surface behind the pencil. He does this quietly and without notice.

The wild hand movements, you see, have distracted the audience's attention. So it looks as though nothing whatsoever is making the pencil move—nothing except the summoning of mental powers and a lot of ridiculous arm waving and finger circles. Practice by yourself—then go find someone to astound.

In the event your mind is not strong enough to move a pencil, forget about the pencil and use a cigarette. Cigarettes are a lot lighter than pencils; don't strain your mind unnecessarily.

TAKING OFF YOUR VEST
WITHOUT TAKING OFF
YOUR COAT

A show-off is truthful, and to tell the truth, fellow show-offs, we don't feel like giving you the hard sell on this one. Oh, we could invent scenarios, pointing out terrific opportunities for self-display, invoking hordes of admiring beauties, jealous athletes and envious international spies. But if you don't immediately see the tremendous opportunities in knowing how to take off your vest without taking off your coat, you're simply not the show-off we took you for.

Here's how it's done. Unbutton your jacket and your vest (if you hoped we'd show you how to do it with both buttoned, we're sorry, because that's impossible). All right, now reach down and grab the left-hand corner of your jacket and stuff it into the left armhole of your vest (figure 1, page 172).

Keep on stuffing the material of your coat into your vest through the left armhole until you can't manage any more. Only then slip your left arm and shoulder—fully clothed with your jacket—out of the vest (figure 2). This will be a little bit awkward, but not impossible. Just go easy and don't tear anything; if it doesn't seem to be working, calm down and fuss with it until things go smoothly.

Once you've got your left arm free, reach around behind and pull more of your coat through that left armhole of the vest. As the coat passes through the vest, the vest passes across your back toward your right shoulder. When you've gone about as far as you can go, bring your right shoulder and arm (and the jacket that's on them both) through the armhole of the vest (figure 3). Once again, take it easy. If you find yourself totally confused, take the whole thing off and start again. If you've done everything right, you are now wearing the vest on your right shoulder only, sort of flopping down your side under the jacket.

Finally, using your left hand, grab some loose vest near the shoulder and stuff it into your right coat sleeve from the inside. Keep pushing your vest into your right sleeve until you can reach some of the vest from the other end of the sleeve—the hand end, that is. When that's possible, just reach into the sleeve from the outside, grab the vest, and pull it out through the sleeve (figure 4).

Now, if you've done it right, your coat is still one hundred percent on, and your vest is one hundred percent off. If you want to learn this the easy way, find a friend who will stand still while you do it to him; after you see from the outside exactly how it works, you'll find it easier to do to yourself. Of course, your clothes get a little rumpled up this way and may need to be pressed afterwards, but we never promised you a thornless rose garden, did we?

HOW TO RECEIVE
BRAIN MESSAGES

This book can show you lots of ways to exploit the real world for your personal glory. This feat will show you how to exploit the unreal world. The dandy psychic experiment below will mystify your most cynical acquaintances. All you need is a telephone directory, a pencil, a piece of paper. And, of course, your own finely tuned extra-sensory-perception (heh, heh). But before you go any further, get out the phone book and turn to page 89. Memorize the tenth name from the top of the far-right column on that page. Now go find your subject.

Tell your subject to write down any three digits, no two of which can be the same. Now tell him to reverse the order of these numbers. In figure 1, the subject has chosen 742 (which in reverse

is 247). Now tell the subject to subtract the smaller figure from the larger.

Ask the subject if he is left with three digits. If he has only two digits, tell him to put a zero in front of them.

Tell your subject to take the result of what he has just subtracted and reverse the numbers. In figure 2, for instance, 495 is reversed to 594. Tell your subject to add these together. The sum is 1089.

The sum is *always* 1089, no matter what three numbers were picked at the outset. And that's how this all works. Ask the subject to turn to the page in the phone book designated by his last two numbers (89). Tell him to count down from the top the number of names designated by the first two digits (10). Tell him to concentrate on this name.

You make a big deal about trying to receive his brain waves. Then tell him what the first name is —now the last. You've had it memorized all along, remember? Your subject will fall down dead!

BLOWING SMOKE RINGS

This peaceful, quiet classic is useful for a small group of intimate friends, or just one friend, if that's all you have. It conveys the impression of thoughtfulness; whenever you blow smoke rings you look as though you were thinking of something else—maybe something important (lots of luck).

It is useful to know that pipe or cigar smoke works better than cigarette smoke, though cigarette smoke will do if there are no drafts in the room. It's not necessary to inhale in order to blow wonderful rings; it's better all around, in fact, if you don't. Inhaled smoke is less dense than non-inhaled smoke and doesn't hang together as well when pushed out of the mouth toward the ceiling. To blow smoke rings, light up and then follow these steps:

1. Draw in enough smoke to fill your mouth. Try to keep it toward the back of your mouth so it won't escape until you want it to.

2. Purse your lips into a tiny, perfectly round O. Rest your tongue lightly on the floor of your mouth. Keep all muscles relaxed.

3. Without changing the shape of the O, increase its size by pulling your upper lip tightly against your upper teeth and dropping your lower jaw slightly. The O at this stage should be about an inch in diameter.

4. Push out the ring by gently flicking your tongue. The back of the tongue is what does the trick; at no time should you stick your tongue out of your mouth. Each mouthful of smoke yields four or five puffy smoke rings. Pause briefly between rings so that one air-current doesn't interfere with the next.

YOUR BASIC
JEW'S HARP INSTRUCTION

Once upon a time, before the transistor radio, just about every kid in America had a Jew's harp (so called for being a leading article of peddler's merchandise in the nineteenth century, but now sometimes sold as the Mouth Harp). Today you can show off with a Jew's harp merely by owning one, for very few people under forty even know what one looks like.

The Jew's harp is a simple lyre-shaped piece of steel with a vibrating reed between its two ends (see figure 1). It is extremely useful for showing off at parties because it can be easily carried in a shirt pocket, because it's easy to play, and because you can just about count on nobody else having one. Yet they are available at any big music store. A word of caution: don't buy a small, cheap, tinny instrument. The big ones are cheap enough, goodness knows, and work a lot better. Now, here's how to play it:

Hold the big end in your left hand and place the two legs flat against your teeth. The hooked end of the reed should point away from your face. Now open your mouth wide enough so the reed, which you're going to pluck in a minute, can pass

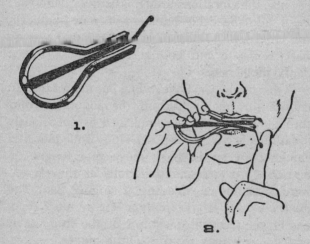

between your teeth on the backswing. Close your lips on the instrument just enough to hold it in place firmly against your teeth without a lot of pressure from the left hand (figure 2).

Ready? Pluck the end of the reed with your right index finger. If you're doing everything right, you should hear a rich harmonious twang. If you fail to hear music at this point you may be doing something wrong like:

1. Biting the instrument. This presses the legs together so the reed hits them with a clank.

2. Not opening your teeth wide enough. If the reed actually strikes your teeth, you get an ugly whacking rattle that hurts.

3. Not maintaining firm contact between your teeth and the body of the instrument. If you just hold it with your lips the sound is dull and muffled, because the vibrations aren't passing through your teeth into the echo-chambers of your skull. On the other hand, don't press so hard that you do nasty things to your teeth; a show-off doesn't need dental problems.

O.K., so now you have a tone but not a tune. To control the pitch, close off the bottom of your throat (this can be accomplished by consciously breathing through your nose). Now, while plucking rhythmically on the reed, move your tongue up and down in your mouth exactly as though you were humming or whistling or singing. See? The pitch changes. It takes only a few minutes' practice to get reasonable control of the intonation; perfect pitch may require a little longer.

Anything you can whistle, you can play on the Jew's harp. The conventional way to strum is in a rapid rhythm, treating everything like a banjo tune, plinky-plink, plinky-plink, but you can slow down for ballads and spirituals. "Boing-boing" effects are particularly easy and satisfying. And for a rich (but tonally uncontrollable) bass pedal-point, open your throat and let the whole column of air right down to your lungs resonate. From here on out, you'll be the life of every party. You could be almost as much fun with a banjo, but people would be able to see you and your banjo-case coming a mile away; with a handy pocket-size Jew's harp, nobody knows you're about to start showing off until it's too late.

WHAT MAKES
SAMMY HUSTLE?

If there's a pool table in your basement, or if you're old and brave enough to make an occasional stop down at your town's billiard emporium, what follows will be of great help to you.

There are two ways to show off at pool. The first is to be able to actually *play* pool, to run a string of fifty balls while your opponent stands there with his teeth in his mouth. The second way is to possess a bit of wit and a touch of sneak. Well, nice to meet you. Here are a couple of neat feats you can pull when it's your opponent who gets hot and you're the one standing there with your teeth in your mouth.

Our first maneuver is sinking a wine glass in an end pocket. This should be practiced in private before it is attempted for an audience. Any wine

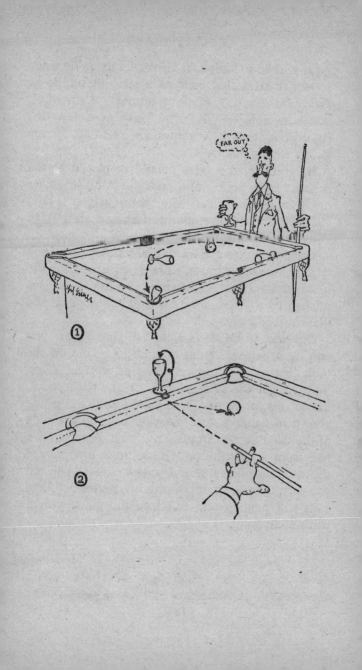

glass will do so long as it curves on the table when rolled. A glass that rolls in a straight line is no good. Once you've made a number of attempts, you'll be able to place the glass at exactly the right spot. Figure 1 shows an example of one glass's rolling habits.

In practice, the glass should be placed at the mouth of the pocket and pushed with your finger *away* from the pocket. The spot at which it consistently stops is the spot you should start from when actually performing.

Once you have a glass that can be trusted, stick with it. One thing to remember: when pushing the glass with your finger, always push firmly. A glass pushed by a finger that slips off the edge of the glass will go awry.

Our second hustle is this. Tell your victim you can hit a ball with your cue, strike a coin on the table, then drive that coin into an upright glass. You can use the same glass as in the trick above. To do this, place the glass on the table's edge, as shown in figure 2, and put your coin on the edge of the table, just in front of the glass. Now strike a ball from across the table in a direct line toward the coin and glass. Some practice shots will tell you how strong to hit. Correctly performed, the coin will pop up and fall into the glass with a triumphant ping.

A NEW TRICK
FOR AN OLD BOTTLE

The difficult the show-off does immediately; the impossible, even faster than that. This impossible stunt requires, by way of materials, an empty soda or beer bottle (or any other kind of bottle with a small top, small enough that a quarter won't fall through), a newspaper, and a pocketful of change.

Assuming you have these things, just look around for someone who doesn't sufficiently respect your powers. When you find him, ask him to watch while you cut (or tear; scissors are helpful but not absolutely necessary) a strip about a foot long and an inch wide from the newspaper. Lay it across the bottle top. Then stack some odd change—say a quarter, a nickel, a dime and maybe a penny—on top of the paper strip and the bottle

top. Ready? Now dare your victim to remove the paper and leave the coins in place. He is not allowed to touch the bottle or the coins, or permit or cause them to be touched by anything. Doesn't look so awfully hard, does it? Let him try. No matter how gently he tugs and jiggles at the paper, the coins will inevitably cascade off in a jingle of failed hopes. He may try pulling the paper out in one grand jerk; same result. He may light the paper with a match, hoping to burn it out; but the best he'll get is a circle of scorched paper, still firmly in place under the coins.

All right, now it's your turn. Exhibit your superiority in the following manner: without touching either the bottle or the coins, cut or tear one end of the paper right across, as close to the bottle-top as possible (see the dotted line in the drawing? closer than that, even, if you can).

Your victim may object at this point: "You didn't say I could cut the paper." The correct reply to that is: "I didn't say you couldn't." Look smug as you answer.

Then, grasp the other end of the paper—the one you didn't cut off—and hit the paper strip a sharp whack with your free hand, or the side of the scissors, or something, midway between the end you're holding and the bottle top. Zip! out comes the paper, leaving the coins and bottle exactly as they were. How come? Because the inertia of the coins is sufficient to resist the friction of the paper for the split second necessary to get the paper out of there. You now have the paper in one hand, and the coins resting firmly on the bottle. You have conquered. Open another bottle and enjoy the glory that is yours.

ACKNOWLEDGMENTS

For the following contributions sent by our far-flung friends and correspondents, the authors of this book are truly grateful—so grateful that we are putting their names right here, in actual print. Mothers of our correspondents, please join with us in recognition of your exhibitionist offspring.

Bob Brown (How to make custom-made money)
Mr. and Mrs. A. Delcorio (How to be calculating)
Priscilla Eakeley (How to be a twenty-card wizard)
J.O. Ferrell (How to be very, very incombustible)
Marjorie Kanehl (Two tricks for a buck)
Bette Palmer (Whistling through grass)
Dominic Valentine (Testing your strength)

We are also grateful to *Esquire's* contributing editor Philip Nobile, in real life an acquisitions editor for Sheed & Ward, who introduced us to his boss, after which things got moving real quick.

ABOUT THE AUTHORS

Tom Ferrell and Lee Eisenberg, coauthors of the nationally syndicated column *The Show-Off*, are both residents of New York and editors at *Esquire* magazine.

Tom Ferrell, managing editor at *Esquire* magazine, graduated from Stanford University. He joined *Esquire* in 1966 as a Ph.D. dropout from Harvard. He was born in Joplin, Missouri.

Lee Eisenberg, senior editor at *Esquire,* was born in Philadelphia in 1946, and received his B.A. and M.A. degrees from the University of Pennsylvania. He lectures at New York University. His work has appeared in *Rolling Stone, The New York Times Book Review* and *National Review.*